PRACTICAL TRUTH

PRACTICAL TRUTH

For Encouragement, Guidance and Hope In This Life
AND To Prepare You For The Next

GEOFFREY CRUZEN GUY

WESTBOW
PRESS
A DIVISION OF THOMAS NELSON

Scripture taken from the New King James Version. Copyright 1979, 1980, 1982 by Thomas Nelson, Inc. Used by permission. All rights reserved.

WestBow Press books may be ordered through booksellers or by contacting:

WestBow Press
A Division of Thomas Nelson
1663 Liberty Drive
Bloomington, IN 47403
www.westbowpress.com
1-(866) 928-1240

Because of the dynamic nature of the Internet, any Web addresses or links contained in this book may have changed since publication and may no longer be valid. The views expressed in this work are solely those of the author and do not necessarily reflect the views of the publisher, and the publisher hereby disclaims any responsibility for them.

ISBN: 978-1-4497-0399-8 (sc)
ISBN: 978-1-4497-0398-1 (dj)
ISBN: 978-1-4497-0446-9 (e)

Library of Congress Control Number: 2010933031

Printed in the United States of America

WestBow Press rev. date: 11/11/2010

CONTENTS

To Niki and Baines, my beloved children. You two are my inspiration for this work and all that I do. As I sought to learn God's truth, I hoped that in so learning, I would learn how to love you more dearly and completely. You guys are my heart. Thank you for simply being.

Acknowledgements

Whenever I used to read acknowledgements at the beginning of a book, I always thought them to be a little sappy and gratuitous. However, now that I've written this book, I understand the emotion and gratitude of those authors. No piece of literature can be an exclusively individual achievement. Even this one, which I've written alone, has the fingerprints of others throughout its pages. Therefore, I would like to offer my sincere thank you to a select few who have been my inspiration and support.

First and foremost, I want to give my most heartfelt thanks to my Lord and Savior Jesus Christ. Lord, I didn't see this one coming. But by Your inspiration and through Your grace, You've allowed me to share words of love and truth to those who will hear Your voice and receive Your truth in their hearts and minds. Thank You, Lord, for loving me and trusting me to be Your voice in these pages. I know that Your word never comes back void but always bears fruit. You are amazing to me, both in Your love and Your grace. I pray that many lives will be touched by these words. Thank You.

Next come my children. They didn't even know I was writing this, but they are my reason for the efforts in this book. As all books do, this one required hundreds of long, lonely hours to research and write. But Niki and Baines, it was my thoughts of you two that kept me going during the times when I was tired or discouraged. People like you make this world a better place in which to live. I hope you enjoy this book, and I pray that God's truth will remain in your hearts always, as you remain in mine.

To Mary, the dear mother of my children. Thank you for loving and nurturing Niki and Baines so very well during the times when I fell short as a father. Most of who and what they've become is due to your tireless, dedicated efforts. You're a great mom; you can take pride in the fruits of your labors. Thank you, Mary.

This book was born while I was enjoying a kindness extended to me by my very dear friend, Barbara, whom I affectionately refer to as "Q." Thank you for allowing me to find my truth in that beautiful place of solitude, your lake house. Barbara, you know that I owe you more than words can say at this time. Thank you for being there when I needed you. You are truly a blessing in my life.

Last, but certainly not least, to my pastor. Pastor, you have kept me grounded when I was heading off in a wrong direction. Your love and friendship have affected me deeply. Your peace in the Lord has been a light to me when I suffered my moments of doubt and insecurity. You've never wavered in your faith, and that has been my anchor. Thank you for being a man of great, unshakeable faith. I love you, my brother in Christ.

†

Introduction

A Good Place To Start

Dear reader, hello, and welcome to this discussion of truth. The truth of which I will be speaking is the truth of God, as revealed in His word, the Holy Bible. As I was beginning to write this book on truth, I was thinking about the fact that in our world, there are many ideas, concepts, traditions, doctrines, etc., that are considered to be "truths." However, as I thought about them, it quickly became apparent that many of those "truths" conflicted with one another. Obviously, that is a problem. Two opposing positions on the same issue cannot both be true. Somewhere there has to be a bottom line, the real, true truth. I believe that bottom line is the word of God. Therefore, all the truths that I will be discussing with you originate from God's word. Opinion, conjecture, and guesswork have all been eliminated.

If you accept the word of God as being true, then you'll enjoy our discussion of the many aspects of God's truth that we'll explore. If you don't believe that God's word is the truth, I hope you'll read on anyhow. At the very least, you will gain an understanding of what God has to say about many things. And perhaps you will even come to believe that God's word is in fact the actual truth. Either way, I think you'll find this to be an interesting read. I've tried to present these ideas and concepts in a fairly light, conversational style. I personally don't like dry, lecture-type material, and I don't think I could write this in that way anyhow. So let's take this journey together, and hopefully in the end, you will agree with me that we are exploring the absolute, undeniable, infallible, unquestionable truth.

In this book, I've quoted many Scripture verses. Unless otherwise noted, all verses are from the Life Application Study Bible NKJV Tyndale House Publishers, Inc.

I don't know how it came to be that you're reading these words, but nevertheless, here you are. Perhaps someone gave this book to you, maybe you picked it up because you're just curious, or perhaps certain aspects of your life may not be going as well as you had hoped and you are searching for some answers. Whatever the reason, I'm glad you're here. Together, we can explore the truth of God, the truth that can set you free.

My purpose in writing this book is fairly simple. I want to give you hope and encouragement in your life. As I've been writing, I've found myself becoming more and more encouraged as I've researched God's word for this book. Far too many people have to deal with all sorts of issues in their lives that are completely unnecessary and that in many cases could have been avoided, if they had known some basic truths—truths about life, themselves, and their God.

It's been said that knowledge is power, and I believe that is true. It is my sincere hope that as you read this book, you will find it useful as a resource to help you gain power to overcome problems, obstacles, and situations in your life. There is a lot of comfort to be gained from God's word, especially if you happen to be dealing with matters of the heart. The love of God is available to all of us if we just open our hearts and minds to receive it. As you learn or re-learn these godly truths, they will give you the knowledge and confidence that you need to meet all the challenges of your life with assurance in your ability to prevail over them. Further, I hope that as you increase in knowledge, you will gain wisdom. Wisdom is the ultimate goal.

For this reason we also … do not cease to pray for you,
and to ask that you may be filled with the knowledge of His will
in all wisdom and spiritual understanding
Colossians 1:9

If you are unsure about God or if you are just considering and investigating Christianity, I hope that in these pages, you will find the answers to your questions about who God is and how His truth can have meaning in your life.

I feel that gaining knowledge and understanding of God's truth is particularly important today, possibly more so than ever before. This may well be the most difficult time to be alive in all of human history. Sure, we've got all kinds of modern technological advantages that past generations didn't have, but we've also got many, many more ways to fall into trouble. With the birth of the Internet came unlimited access to anything and everything that we could possibly want, and a lot of things that we don't want or need. The pace of our lives is so fast, and the demands on our minds are so intense, that we're forced to operate at unnatural levels of mental activity. The stress on our minds is taking a serious toll on our mental and emotional well being. We've lost sight of how to relax, slow down, handle the important things, and let the rest be. We have become a society of people who sweat the small stuff and fail to recognize the big stuff. We've gained scientifically and intellectually, but we've declined morally and spiritually. As we seek to explore new intellectual frontiers in our collective search for new knowledge, we're losing our moral compass and core values. The principles that our forefathers embraced are being discarded as old fashioned and irrelevant, and that fact is causing great internal conflict within many of us. When God created us, He gave us a spirit nature, and He put an awareness of His will and His standards of morality in our hearts and minds. We know that awareness as our "conscience"; that still, small voice that speaks to us when we are faced with particular situations and choices.

> ... says the Lord: "I will put My laws into their hearts,
> and in their minds I will write them"
> Hebrews 10:16

It is no wonder so many of us are having so many problems. We are trying to live against our very nature. We were not created as godless beings, but that is how many of us are trying to live. It cannot work. We cannot deny ourselves. William Shakespeare said: "This above all: to thine own self be true." He was so very right. When we try to be what we are not, we encounter all manner of problems, both within ourselves and with others. If we are to live peacefully and successfully, we must be true to who and what we are—children of God.

I believe in this book, you will find the answers that you are seeking—not because of me and what I have written, but because of the source behind the truths I'm going to discuss—Almighty God, the author of Truth, the Creator of you, me, and everything. What I've written is not my opinion or my theory. This book is a distillation of truth-filled verses from the word of God—the Holy Bible, the ultimate source of truth. I believe God will use the verses I've chosen to share with you to teach you the practical truths that will help you to overcome the problems and situations you face in your daily life. When you understand, appreciate, and incorporate the truth of God into your life, you can do much more than just survive in this life; you can thrive in it.

The Bible is God's gift to us. It is His manual for how we are to live, so that we can enjoy lives that are happy, fulfilling, successful, and full of abundant love for God, for ourselves, and for one another.

As you read this book, you may say to yourself, *I know this stuff. I've heard it before.* Of course you have; God's truth has been around since long before you and me. Yes, you may have heard it, but apparently, you didn't get it. You, like me and so many others, have somehow missed at least part of the message of God's truth. That fact may well be some of the reason why you're struggling in your life right now. But as you've probably heard, God works in mysterious ways. For one thing, He's put this book in your hands. You may not have been thinking about Him, but He is thinking about you. He is leading you to the truth that can transform you back into the man or woman He created you to be. As you discover, or re-discover, the beauty and wisdom of God's truth, you can begin to live the life you were created to live – the life that God planned for you.

> "For I know the plans I have for you," declares the Lord,
> "plans to prosper you and not to harm you,
> plans to give you hope and a future."
> Jeremiah 29:11

I don't know where you are in life. Maybe things are going great for you; maybe they're not. If they are, congratulations. You are fortunate and blessed. However, if your life is not going so well, then you're like a lot of us. Life is tough, and it is not getting any easier. We are all fighting some kind of battles. Some are big, some are little, but always, to each of us, they are personal. No one knows your battles but you and God. Sometimes I'm sure you feel as though you have to fight them all alone. I am pleased to tell you that you are mistaken. You do not ever have to be alone in your life or your battles. You can have the greatest general in history—Jesus Christ—fighting beside you, protecting you against any and all enemies you will ever face. All you need to do is ask Him, and He will be there. He told us plainly:

And whatever things you ask in prayer, believing, you will receive
Matthew 21:22

I am with you always, even to the end of the age.
Matthew28:20

If you are currently experiencing unrest in your life, I'd like to take this moment to offer you a blessing. I am going to present to you some of the most soothing and reassuring words that you will ever read. They've helped me during some difficult times, and I'm certain they can help you right now. Relax for a moment and let these words bathe you in God's loving assurance.

The LORD is my shepherd;
I shall not want.
He makes me to lie down in green pastures;
He leads me beside the still waters.
He restores my soul;
He leads me in the paths of righteousness for His name's sake.
Yea, though I walk through the valley of the shadow of death,
I will fear no evil;
For You are with me;
Your rod and Your staff, they comfort me.

You prepare a table before me in the presence of my enemies;
You anoint my head with oil;
My cup runneth over.
Surely goodness and mercy shall follow me
All the days of my life;
And I will dwell in the house of the LORD Forever.
Psalm 23

Now, don't you feel more relaxed, perhaps a little more confident, having just read those words? When the inevitable trials of life come upon you, take a few moments and meditate on these words. You cannot help but feel calmer and more self-assured. That is the beauty of having God and His Truth in your life. He is always there for you when you need Him. That is the truth—every time, all the time.

On that happy note, let me continue by telling you how this book came about. I was facing many personal challenges. I felt overwhelmed and for the most part, helpless to deal with them. I finally gave up and gave in and turned to the Lord for help.

I kept thinking that life has to make more sense than this. I wondered: *Why do I have so many problems? Why is it so hard for me to find happiness? I know life isn't supposed to be easy, but does it have to be **this** hard?* I was feeling quite desperate. I had been involved in a very serious motor vehicle accident in which I suffered multiple vertebral fractures. I was living with constant, sometimes severe pain, and I was unable to work in the manner to which I was accustomed. As a result, I was becoming stressed and depressed as financial problems were continuing to mount. In addition, my marriage was failing. Everything seemed to be coming apart. Something had to give, before I did. I couldn't get excited about anything. I was just existing, and not well at that.

Finally, I asked a very dear friend of mine if I could go to a house that she owned on a lake to get away for a few days and try to sort things out. When I got there, after spending a few moments looking around at that beautiful place, I got on my knees and cried out to God. I said, *Lord, You know I believe in You and I've prayed to You for many years. I really need Your help now. My life is in such a mess. I don't feel as though I have a purpose for my life. Why am I not getting it? I'm too smart (or so I thought, since I hold a doctorate degree) to have all these problems.*

Then it happened. I heard in my mind a voice as clear as if you, dear reader, were right beside me speaking. "Geoff, you must learn the truth. When you do, you will be free. And when you become free, you will know your purpose." For a few moments, I could scarcely move. I knelt there, kind of stunned, and tears flooded my eyes. God had just spoken to me; I had no doubt. Suddenly I realized that although I still had all my problems, I knew then that I could overcome them. God had just told me how. Many times I had read words that were similar to those that God had just spoken to me.

You shall know the truth, and the truth shall make you free
John 8:32

Sure, I'd read them, but they had never gotten my attention before. I just read them and kept right on reading. I never realized that in those words, was the answer to my life's problems. God had told me, "Learn the truth, and you will be free."

That, as they say, was my "moment of truth." I began reading and studying and asking God to reveal His truth to my heart and mind. But I kept wondering about the free thing. Free? Free how? Free from what? I'll talk about the answer to that in the next chapter.

Right now, let me make one thing perfectly clear. I am not in an exclusive, privileged club with God. You and everyone else on this planet can hear from God. If you will ask God to teach you His Truth and His will for your life, He will open your mind to things you've never imagined.

Unless you, I, or anyone else learns the truth that God has ordained for our lives, we are doomed to struggle needlessly against situations and adversities born of ignorance and misconception. God gave us His word of truth to save us and free us from most of the problems we now face in life. When we ignore His truth, we are left to fend for ourselves in a world that is confusing, hostile, and often dangerous. You must realize that just as we are here to love, teach, and guide our own children through the trials of life, God is here as our Heavenly Father to love, teach, and guide us. He does it by making known to us His truth. He wrote it all down in His manual for our lives—the Holy Bible. All we have to do is accept His gift of truth and love, and we can learn to enjoy lives of love, peace, and joy heretofore unknown to us.

One of my favorite sayings is, "Be careful what you ask for; you may get it." As I began learning the truth, it became clear to me that God was also giving me my purpose—I am to share His truth with as many people as I can.

When I realized I was supposed to write this book, I wondered if I could do it. I've never authored anything before, except some professional papers and a few short articles. Then I thought, *Geoff, are you kidding? If God wants you to write a book for Him, He will give you the ability.* I recalled a Scripture in which Jesus was telling His disciples not to worry about what they would say when they went to preach about Him, because He would give them the words.

> Do not worry about ... what you should say.
> "For the Holy Spirit will teach you in that
> very hour what you ought to say"
> Luke 12:11-12

I said to myself, *Okay, then, I'm going to trust you, Lord, to give me the words so people can receive the message of Your truth.* And that, dear reader, is the how and why of this book. In writing this, I've tried very hard to be faithful in delivering the message that He intended.

It's no accident that you're reading this right now. Make no mistake, God has chosen this moment to speak to you. He is calling you to learn the truth because He is preparing you to do His will in something. He gives each of us His word to get us ready to be His agents here on earth. His word is given to teach us:

> For the equipping of the saints for the work of ministry
> Ephesians 4:12

Don't get nervous. That verse doesn't mean you have to go into the ministry as you think of the traditional definition of ministry. It just means that God has a purpose for your life, and if you'll allow Him, He will work through you to facilitate His eternal plan. Perhaps you didn't realize that your life is a ministry of sorts. Well it is. You cannot live without having some kind of effect on others. Whether you use your life for good or evil is up to you, but by your existence, others will be influenced in some way. I pray that you will ask God to make known to you His will for your life, so that you can become a light in the world. This world certainly needs more light; the darkness is pervasive. Jesus gave this command to all of us.

Let your light so shine before men, that
they may see your good works
and glorify your Father in heaven.
Matthew 5:16

That is actually the overall purpose for all of our lives. Each of us is to play a specific part in God's plan. I hope you will ask God to disclose His plan to you—your specific role in the grand scheme of things. If you are thinking, *I don't know anything about how to work for God. I wouldn't even know where to start,* don't worry, no one knows at first. God will teach you. God is not looking for your ability; He is looking for your availability.

God will never ask you to do anything without giving you whatever is required for you to complete the task. Whether you'll require words, courage, compassion, strength, or knowledge, God will equip you. He will never lead you into a situation unarmed. I don't know what He has in store for you, but He is ready to begin working His purpose in your life. Your job is simply to show up and be willing. If you're getting nervous, just relax. God may be asking you to do something as natural as caring for an aging parent or maybe to volunteer at your child's school. Any life lived in the will of God is a ministry, so don't worry that you're going to have to be some kind of a Jesus freak.

I believe there is built into each of us the need and desire to experience God in our lives. He created us. He left His mark on us—in our hearts. Deep inside, we all sense that there is some power greater than ourselves. We inherently know there is more to our existence and this universe than just us. Without realizing it, we seek after it. When we are in trouble, we instinctively cry out, just as does a child. We may not even realize it, but we are crying out to our Creator, our Heavenly Father. That is what He wants from us,

His children. He wants to love us, and He wants us to love Him and depend on Him for our lives.

If you are a parent, then you can imagine the frustration God must feel with us sometimes. From the beginning, His children have given Him trouble. He created Adam and Eve, and He gave them an entire magnificent planet for them to enjoy and utilize its resources as they pleased. He gave them unlimited freedom, with the exception of only one rule to obey—don't eat from one particular tree. Well, of course, you know what they did. Sound at all similar to your own kids? I'd like to say, if you are having problems with your kids, don't get discouraged, it could be worse. Do you recall what happened with God's grandkids? One of them killed the other. God's been through a lot with us. But you know what? He still loves us, and He still wants to give us great and wonderful blessings. We simply need to listen to Him as our Heavenly Father and trust Him and follow His guidance. If we are willing to listen and live by the truth He has given us, He will make us free to live lives that are better than we could ever plan for ourselves. God wants us to possess and experience the qualities of happiness, peace, joy, and love. When we possess those qualities, or perhaps I should say, when they possess us, we will become truly free to enjoy this curious, unpredictable, often breathtaking, sometimes heartbreaking journey that we know as life.

To many of you, some of these truths that I will be discussing may seem so obvious, so simple as to be almost foolish. Don't be deceived by their apparent simplicity. The Bible says:

The foolishness of God is wiser than men
1Corinthians 1:25

As we begin our exploration of truth, I want to give you a snapshot of myself so hopefully, you will feel comfortable with me as I talk to you. It is my desire that this book will feel like a conversation between us. I've debated with myself about including this information, but the more I thought about it, the more it seemed relevant. Many times when I've read something, and read the little bio about the author, he or she seemed to be living a life that was too successful or too charmed for me to be able to relate to him or her.

It's important for you to know that I'm just like you. I'm an ordinary man, living a fairly ordinary life. I've experienced some wonderfully happy moments, and I've endured many of the hardships that are all too common in our modern society. Along the way, I've won some and I've lost some. I've been blessed with two amazing children who are now wonderful young adults. (They are at the top of my win column!) I've suffered the heartache of divorce, and I've had financial problems due to poor business decisions, the most prominent being my premature decision to retire from my private practice as a Chiropractic Physician. It was a few months before I began writing this book, when I had my automobile accident. Despite my permanent pain, when I consider what could have happened to me, I feel very blessed. I used to wonder why God spared me in that accident. But since my trip to the lake house, I now believe it's because He has work for me to do for Him, this book being part of that work. All the ups, downs, and arounds of my life were simply to prepare me for now.

I would like to add a qualifying note about this book. It is not a pie in the sky, life is a bowl of cherries kind of book. It's about truth, and the truth is, life is tough. Sometimes, it's awfully tough. That's reality; that's the truth. You see, we were never promised a pain-free, stress-free life. In fact, we were promised just the opposite. But we were also promised help and a way out of our problems. Jesus said:

In this world you will have tribulation...
John 16:33

However, He did not say we had to be defeated or miserable because of it. In fact, His statement continues:

... But be of good cheer, I have overcome the world
John 16:33

In the book of Philippians, we are told:

I can do all things through Christ who strengthens me.
Philippians 4:13

The writer of Hebrews wrote:

For He Himself has said, "I will never leave you nor forsake you"
Hebrews 13:5

If we trust God with our lives, He will be there with us and He will get us through anything and everything. But if you still find yourself worrying, look at these words of truth and love that Jesus spoke about worrying.

Therefore I say to you, do not worry about your life,
What you will eat or what you will drink;
Nor about your body, what you will put on ...
For your heavenly Father knows that you need all these things.
But seek first the kingdom of God and His righteousness,
And all these things shall be added to you.
Matthew 6:25-33

Remember what Jesus said:

I am the way, the truth, and the life.
John 14:6

Jesus cannot speak anything but the truth, because He *is* the Truth. He said you need not worry, so stop worrying. Replace worry with Faith—faith in the God who created you and who loves you. Believe in the truth of God and you will find that your perspective on life in general and your life in particular, will begin to change for the better. Normally, I would say trust me on this. But instead, I'll say trust God and His word on this.

When you choose to put your faith in God and His word, you can rest in the assurance that He, your Heavenly Father, will provide for all your needs if you ask in His name, according to His will for your life.

Ask, and it will be given to you; seek, and you will find;
knock and it will be opened to you.
Matthew 7:7

As you open your heart and mind to acquire an understanding of the truths we will be discussing, you will begin to appreciate their wisdom and beauty, and they will enrich your life. So, if you're ready, let's go right on into it, shall we?

✝

TRUTH

It Will Set You Free

You shall know the truth,
and the truth shall make you free
John 8:32

What is truth, and how does it make us free? We've got two issues here, Truth and Freedom. I will start with Truth, and then I'll address Freedom.

Man has pondered and sought after truth since he drew his first breath eons ago. Truth is elusive, invisible, and intangible. We can't see truth, or touch it. It's not accessible to our five senses, yet it is essential to our lives. So what is truth?

Truth is that which is absolute;
it is not subject to interpretation, belief or question.

Truth is reliable; it withstands all scrutiny.

Truth is consistent; it never changes.

Truth is eternal; it has always been, and always will be.

Truth is the window to the mind of God.

Why is truth important to us? Man, even in his limited wisdom, realized early on that truth is necessary for the existence of civilization. Without truth, agreements would not endure, and business could not be transacted with any expectation of success. In our courts of law, truth is the only hope of justice; witnesses are sworn to tell the truth, the whole truth, and nothing but the truth. Relationships would be meaningless without the promise of truth between individuals. Truth is the cornerstone on which all of mankind's institutions are built. A government without truth in its design is doomed for collapse. Society without truth quickly degrades into anarchy. Outside of truth, there exists only chaos. Ultimately, our lives and our well-being depend on truth.

The Bible tells us:

"For this is good and acceptable in the sight of God our Savior,
Who desires all men to be saved and to come
to the knowledge of the truth"
1Timothy 2:3-4

All truth comes from our Creator—God. He created truth out of His love for us. Through the truth of His word, God has given us the blueprint for how we should live our lives. He knows that many snares and temptations await us on our journey through life, and without His word to guide us, we will be vulnerable to self-inflicted disaster. In effect, God gave us His truth to save us from ourselves. Sadly, many people reject His truth, and their lives reflect the consequences of that choice.

I think many people struggle with trusting and believing in God, simply because we can't prove Him. We have become such a science and logic based people that if we can't prove something by eyewitness or physical evidence proof, then we don't accept it. I know because I went through the same thought process, especially when I was in college studying marine biology. Everything I was involved in was based on scientific proof. Even though I had been taught the gospel as a child, I was so enmeshed in the science mindset that God just didn't seem to fit.

We must take God on faith. However, therein lies the rub for most people. Sometimes the notion that people don't or won't take God on faith seems absurd to me. Just look around you at this amazing world, and observe all of Creation. Can you really believe all this happened by chance or accident? By default, the evidence for God is overwhelming. When I think about it, it seems that it takes more faith to deny God's existence and believe in our existence by random chance.

It's funny, but despite what I said a moment ago about science training me to demand evidential proof, it was during the most intense period of my scientific training, my medical training, that I began to realize the truth of God's existence. We are so perfectly made, in such exquisite, intricate detail that I became convinced there had to be a mind of unfathomable intelligence behind all this. I came to realize that God's word is true; you can accept it and rely on it. You can bet your life on it. Actually, as you will see, *you are betting your life on it*—your eternal life.

"And the truth shall make you free"

Free to do what?

The truth of God will set you free to live the life that He intended for you to live when He created you. With God's truth as your map, and His will as your compass, your steps will be directed by God as He leads you into your own personal "promised land" according to His plan.

Free from what?

Free from living the kind of life that Henry David Thoreau described when he said, "Most men lead lives of quiet desperation." You can be free from the bondage of living under the influences and effects of untruth in your life. Free from such ideas as, "I'm not worthy. I'm not lovable. I'm a failure. I'll never be happy." Most, if not all, of people's problems and unhappiness stem from believing these and similar untruths, and then subconsciously letting themselves and their potential be limited by them.

Of course you'll be unhappy if you believe you're not lovable. And of course you'll be unsuccessful if you believe you're a failure, and on and on … But all those ideas are not true. They are horrible, crippling lies. They fester in your mind until you've accepted them as being true. Then they exert their influence in your life and render you unable to live up to your true God-given and God-intended potential. Actually, it comes down to an identity crisis. You've been brainwashed into believing that you are someone or something that you are not—a failure, an unlovable person, etc.

The truth is that you are a child of God. You were created in His image—a perfect being with unlimited potential.

> For You formed my inward parts;
> You covered me in my mother's womb.
> I will praise You, for I am fearfully and wonderfully made
> Psalm 139

If you will allow me a moment of poor grammar, there's an old saying that fits well here: "God don't make no junk." Dear reader, you are nothing less than a perfectly made, flawlessly beautiful creation that was lovingly designed by Almighty God, the Creator of the universe.

> The very hairs of your head are all numbered
> Matthew 10:30

> Therefore humble yourselves under the mighty hand of God,
> that He may exalt you in due time, casting all
> your care upon Him, for He cares for you
> 1Peter 5:6-7

Every inch of you matters to God. If you think any less of yourself, you are selling yourself short and are insulting God for His creation—you. He values you very highly; learn to value yourself. Only by allowing the infiltration of false, limiting ideas into your consciousness have you become less than what God intended for you to be. However, you can reclaim your true identity and reprogram yourself back into who and what God designed you to be by learning His truth for your life.

Where do you find God's truth? You find it in His word, the Holy Bible. As I've been researching the Bible for this "conversation," I've been reminded just how true it is that the answers for just about any issue in your life can be found in the word of God.

I had always thought of the Bible as an interesting historical document. It is that, to be sure. But it is also, as I had been told, a living, breathing work that speaks to you and is relevant to your life and the world today. As you get into the word of God, you will find that certain verses will jump out at you and you will have some of those "Aha" moments. If you're like me, you'll find yourself saying, "Wow, this really does address my life situation right now."

The Bible is actually an incredible work that defies all probability. It was written by about forty different writers, who wrote at different times, spanning about fifteen hundred years. And yet, there is an orderly progression of a common theme from beginning to end. That fact alone is almost incomprehensible. The odds of something like that happening by chance are beyond infinitesimally small. That truth argues a common authorship, or inspiration. I firmly believe that the Bible is the divinely inspired word of God. No other explanation makes any sense whatsoever.

I once had a concern about the Bible. After all, it was written by humans, so is it reliable? Scripture answers that question for us.

And so we have the prophetic word confirmed,
which you do well to heed as a light that shines in a dark place,
until the day dawns and the morning star rises in your hearts;
knowing this first, that no prophecy of Scripture is of any private
interpretation, for prophecy never came by the will of man, but
holy men of God spoke as they were moved by the Holy Spirit
2Peter 1:19-21

You may say, *Yes, Geoff, but why should I trust a document that bears witness of itself?* You don't have to blindly trust it. If you want to know the truth, read the Bible yourself. Review the evidence and form your own verdict.

If you want some outside opinions from others who have asked the same questions and have reported the findings of their investigations, there are many excellent texts by authors who have set out to prove or disprove the Bible. One of the best that I know of is

> *The New Evidence that Demands a Verdict* by Josh McDowell. (His first edition was *Evidence that Demands a Verdict*, hence *"The New"* in this most recent edition.)

Two others are

> *The Case for Christ* by Lee Strobel

and *The Historical Reliability of the Gospels* by Dr. Craig Blomberg.

When you decide to accept God's word as being the truth, and you find His will for your life as revealed through His word, you will see changes happening in yourself—in the way you think of yourself, in the way you think of others, in the very things that you think about, and even your pattern of speech. Many of your old, "human" desires will leave you. Your thoughts will be on more "godly" things. You will find yourself becoming kinder, gentler, more patient, more understanding, more compassionate, more sympathetic, more "Christ like." And as you grow in your walk with the Lord, continue to ask Him to reveal His truth to you in everything you do. Follow the lead of King David:

> Show me Your ways, O Lord; Teach me Your paths.
> Lead me in Your truth and teach me,
> For You are the God of my salvation;
> Psalm 25:4-5

You will no longer have to continue to live a life of "quiet desperation." As you walk this journey toward discovery of the truth, you will begin to see solutions for the "hopeless" situations in your life. The impossible will become possible. Doubt will give way to faith. Fear will find courage. Problems will become opportunities.

Obstacles will become lessons. You will find power in yourself that you never imagined.

Am I saying that suddenly life will be a piece of cake for you? Of course not; that is not truth. I am telling you that if you know the truth, when problems do arise, you will be able to deal with those problems in their proper perspective, without letting them rob you of your peace and happiness. Then, as you begin to live in truth, you will find yourself enjoying the life that you've always dreamed of but thought was beyond your reach. That is good news—that is truth!

Out of His love for us, God gave us the freedom to make our own choices. He has allowed us to accept His guidance, or to do it our own way. I've tried both. It may come as no surprise I've learned that God's plan is a lot better than mine. I suspect if you give His plan a try, you'll find that His way is better than yours as well. After all, He made us, and He wrote the instruction manual for our lives. Who can know what's better for the product than the manufacturer?

I can only surmise that people reject God's truth because of their mistaken understanding of the nature of God. People, in their own wisdom, have rejected God's truth because they want to be free. Free for what? To live in the mess they're in now? They think that if they submit to God's plan, they will lose their freedom of choice, their freedom to live their lives as they choose. That's not true. Many people mistake God's principles for God's orders. God always gives you the choice to do as you want. The truth is this: When you live in line with God's principles, He walks with you and blesses you along the way. When you choose to live outside of His principles and walk by yourself, He still loves you, but He lets you go alone on your way, and whatever happens, happens. That's pretty fair, don't you think? God is no different from our earthly parents. When we did what our parents wanted us to do, they were much more likely to step in and help us. When we did things we wanted to do, our parents tended to step back and let us learn from the error of our ways. And like God, our parents hoped that one day we would see the wisdom their experience afforded them and come back to the principles they taught us. But whether we did or we didn't, our parents still love us. So does God. He's just a little sadder when He sees us struggling and suffering because of some of the choices we've made. He only wants what's best for us, and the truth is, He does know what is best for each of us. He can see what lies ahead, whereas we can only guess or imagine what lies ahead.

Have you ever come up with some great plan or idea, and then had roadblocks appear so you couldn't do whatever it was? Pretty frustrating, wasn't it? But later, did something else work out that was better than you had planned? Pretty cool, wasn't it? Guess who put the roadblocks in place, and guess who engineered the new plan. Yes, it was God. He saved you from yourself, and then He gave you what was best for you. It is my sincere hope that as you experience such times, you will begin to realize God really does love you, and that you can trust Him. As you grow to trust Him, you will grow to depend on Him because you will know that He will never let you down. I encourage you to try trusting Him with your life. If you do, you'll open yourself up to limitless possibilities. It really is fun to live with God; you never know what He's got cooking for you.

For many people, including myself, it sometimes takes a long time to realize that God's plan for our lives is pretty good after all. Sadly, for some people, that time never comes. They never accept God's plan, and they just live their lives as they choose from beginning to end. Whatever way you choose to go, God will never deny you that choice. But please understand, He also never denies

Himself the choice to bless us or not, depending on our choices as they relate to His will. What I had to learn was to quit blaming God for my problems when they were due to my decisions, not His. If you choose not to walk with the Lord, then you can't expect Him to be blessing you all the time. Fair is fair, right?

As I look back on my life, I can't help but notice that when I was walking with Him and trusting Him to lead me, my life went pretty well. During the times when I rejected God and His help in my life, I had problems, some quite serious. But through it all, He always let me decide who was going to be in charge. God is a gentleman. He prefers to help us make our beds, but if we insist on making them ourselves, He will let us lie in them. He only asks that we don't complain if we don't like the way the sheets fit.

Now that I've been able to live long enough to look back and clearly see the different episodes of my life and how things worked out, I realize how absurd it was for me to reject God's truth so that I could have my personal freedom. There was just one problem with my concept of freedom; I was not free at all. I was living in the bondage of my own life, with all the mistakes and missteps, stress and worry, and unhappiness and anger at my own inability to get myself out of the messes that I'd gotten myself into.

I didn't find the peacefulness and happiness of true personal freedom until I finally surrendered my life to Jesus and let Him help me get my life straightened out. It didn't happen overnight, but steadily, He has shown me the way to find my peace and my true personal freedom. You know what is really frustrating? Now that I've finally learned and accepted the truth, I wish I hadn't waited so long. I missed a lot of opportunities for blessings and happiness. I see now that I could have avoided a lot of problems—if I had just listened to that still, small voice deep inside me that kept calling me to the Lord.

You see, it doesn't matter when you decide to call on the Lord. He's very patient, He'll wait for you. He's got all the time in the world. But you don't, and I don't; none of us do. Our time is limited. My point is this: I don't want you to make the same mistake I made and waste a lot of time in your life. I want you to get the most out of your lifetime.

Integrity and Doing the Right Thing

While I'm on the subject of truth, I want to briefly talk about something that I feel is extremely important. I will use an example from my own life to illustrate my point. If we are going to try to live *by* the truth, then we must live *as* the truth. We must conduct ourselves with integrity, and we must always try to do the right things.

Dictionary.com gives this definition of integrity: adherence to moral and ethical principles; soundness of moral character; honesty

There was an event that occurred while I was living in San Diego and attending college there. To this day, I regret the choices I made at that time. I've forgiven myself, but I have not forgotten the episode. In the grand scheme of things, it's a relatively small issue, but it was apparently important enough that the lesson learned has stayed with me through the years. One more point that I want to make before I describe the event is this: My decision and my choice at that time was a reflection of my character at that time. I was a selfish, self-absorbed college student who was more interested in myself and what I wanted than what was right for all parties concerned. You may be saying, *Geoff, you're being kind of hard on yourself.* Perhaps, but I want to point out that who we are is evidenced in our behavior—how we conduct ourselves, both in private and in public. I'm telling you this because if you're like most people, which you probably are, then you think you're basically a pretty good person. And you probably are, but are you as good as you can be or as good as you know you should be? Do you always try to do the right thing? Do you try to operate in truth? I'm not trying to be holier-than-thou or critical or judgmental. I have neither right nor room for that. I'm doing for you what I did for myself. I'm holding up the mirror of truth and integrity for you to evaluate yourself. How does your reflection look? I sincerely hope you want to be the best man or woman that you can possibly be, every time, all the time.

Okay, here's what happened. I had just moved back to San Diego to attend San Diego State University. I'm originally from there—Coronado actually. I was driving to a store to get a new television. As I was driving, I thought I saw a wallet lying in the road. I looked back in my rearview mirror, and sure enough, I saw bills literally blowing in the wind. I immediately pulled over, jumped out, and ran back. Bills were flying around like an upside down ticker tape parade. I ran around in the street, dodging cars and grabbing bills as fast as I could. Then I saw the wallet. I picked it up and took off back to my car with my treasure. I went on my way wondering how I had gotten so lucky. I had been able to grab $112. I thought, "Wow, this is great! I just saved $112 on my TV." Of course, I went ahead and bought the TV and took it home. A few days later, my apartment was broken into. My new TV was stolen, as well as my stereo and my camera.

What I didn't realize was that event was a test of who I was. It was a test of my integrity, or the lack thereof. I had failed miserably, and God had sent me an emphatic report card—the break-in and subsequent loss of much more than just the TV.

Here's the kicker. When I jumped back in my car after finding the wallet, I had looked inside it. I saw that it belonged to a professor at my college. I had the choice to put the money back in the wallet and take it to the professor the next day. Instead, I did what I did. I didn't even return the empty wallet, for which I'm sure the professor would have been very grateful.

For everything we do, good or bad, right or wrong, there is always a consequence to either ourselves or to others. That consequence may not always be readily apparent or occur right away. But make no mistake, it will occur. Whatever goes around truly, absolutely, surely does come back around.

Please, dear reader, whenever you are faced with a choice or opportunity for anything, choose to do the right thing, every time, all the time. Whatever immediate, short-term gain may be tempting you to do the wrong thing, believe me, it is not worth it. Even though I've forgiven myself, I still wish I could apologize to that man. But I cannot, because I don't remember his name. He wasn't one of my professors. That event is long past, but it still haunts me because I have not been able to get the closure that an apology would have granted me. No matter how disadvantageous doing the right thing may appear to be at the moment, it is always the *best* thing to do—always!

Back to our main topic: the truth of the Lord is *the* truth. You can look elsewhere for other truths, but ultimately, you will find that they are counterfeits. Somehow, some way, other truths will let you down in the end. As you read through the truths I've presented in this book, I hope that in them, you will find the answers that will help you in your life. That is my purpose in writing this book—to share the truth that has helped me and that I know and believe can help you.

You shall know the truth, and the truth shall make you free.
John 8:32

Therefore if the Son makes you free, you shall be free indeed
John 8:36

✝

IT'S ALL ABOUT JESUS

The All in All

Therefore I also, do not cease to give thanks for you,
making mention of you in my prayers: that
the God of our Lord Jesus Christ,
the Father of glory, may give to you the spirit of
wisdom and revelation in the knowledge of Him, the
eyes of your understanding being enlightened;
that you may know what is the hope of His calling,
what are the riches of the glory of His inheritance in the saints,
and what is the exceeding greatness of His
power toward us who believe,
according to the working of His mighty
power which He worked in Christ
when He raised Him from the dead and
seated Him at His right hand
in the heavenly places, far above all principality and power and might
and dominion, and every name that is named,
not only in this age but also in that which is to come.
And He put all things under His feet, and
gave Him to be head over all things
to the church, which is His body, the
fullness of Him who fills all in all.
Ephesians 1:17-23

That is quite a statement to make about someone. But of course, the Apostle Paul wasn't talking about just anyone. He was speaking of Jesus, the Son of God. With that in mind, no statement could be an overstatement. Jesus is what it's all about. He is truly the Alpha and the Omega, the beginning and the end. Everything that is was created by Him, through Him, and for Him. That includes you and me. If you don't happen to believe that's true right now, perhaps you may change your opinion by the time you've reached the end of this chapter. Or at least hopefully you'll be willing to give it some more thought.

There are three major truths that I want to discuss about Jesus. As you read through this chapter, hopefully you will gain at least a basic understanding of each of them. They are as follows:

1. Jesus is of Divine essence. He is not just a human being.
2. He came to earth to teach us, and to die as a sacrifice for our sins, so that we can, through Him, gain access to eternal life in Heaven.
3. He rose again from the dead to allow His Spirit to live in us and through us in this life.

In short, He came to give His life for us, to give His life to us, so He could live his life through us.

I've wondered how I was going to write this, the most important of all my chapters, about the most important topic in the universe. I think I'll start at the end and go from there—the end of your life, that is. When you arrive at the end of your life, then what? You are going to spend eternity somewhere, but where? The answer to that question is why "It's All About Jesus."

You've probably heard it said that through Jesus, you can have eternal life. I want to clear up a very important point about the issue of eternal life. With or without Jesus, you've already got eternal life. What Jesus does for you is determine your address. With Him, you'll be spending eternity in an extraordinary resort, sitting by the pool enjoying a cool drink. Without Him, you'll be living in the hot desert of misery and despair, begging for a cool drink.

I think it's fair to say that there has never been anyone who has ever lived on our great planet who has generated more discussion, more disagreement, and more controversy than Jesus Christ. During His life, and ever since then, the debate about Him has been endless. Everyone has an opinion, or some sort of feelings about Him. No one is neutral. If you're reading this, and you're not a Christ-follower, you may be thinking, *I'm neutral. I don't care about Him one way or the other.* Really? Are you sure about that?

It's interesting to me that people can enter into a discussion about religion, and if someone mentions the name of Buddha, Mohammed, Allah, the Dali Lama, or some other religious figure, the conversation just goes on without any emotional involvement. However, whenever Jesus is mentioned, there is always an emotional response of some kind. I'm sure you know what I'm talking about. If you think for a moment, you'll realize that you always feel something when someone starts talking about Jesus. You may feel comfort at the mention of His name, or you may feel some sort of uneasiness, but you surely feel something. Curious, isn't it? Why should your, my, or anyone's reaction to the name of Jesus be different from their reaction to any other name? Really, who cares? Apparently everyone, in one way or another. But why? The answer, as you will see, is part of why "It's All About Jesus." More specifically, the answer is in the first of the three truths about Him—He is divine.

I believe people react to the name of Jesus because He is not just another man, not just another great teacher, or prophet. He is much more than that. He is someone we cannot ignore. He is someone who evokes a response so deep that it's visceral, beneath our level of thought. It happens in our spirit. Again, but why? Why would our spirits react to Jesus?

The Gospel of John begins with the verses below.

> In the beginning was the Word, and the Word was with God,
> and the Word was God. He was in the beginning with God.
> All things were made through Him,
> and without Him nothing was made that was made.
> In Him was life, and the life was the light of men
> John 1:1-4

Remember, we are creations of God. He put into us a spirit nature. Our spirit nature is sensitive to other spirits, especially one as powerful as the Spirit of God. The Spirit of God? I thought we were talking about Jesus. We are. Let me repeat part of the verse above.

> In the beginning was the Word, and the Word was with God,
> and the Word was God.
> John 1:1

The "Word" in that verse refers to Jesus. He is the Word, and He is God. That is why we all react to His name. If your spirit is with Him, that is, if you are a believer in Christ, then your reaction to His name is one of peace and comfort, you enjoy hearing His name. If however, you have not accepted Christ as your Savior, if your spirit is not "with" Him, then you will feel discomfort at the sound of His name. Jesus said it very plainly.

> He who is not with Me is against Me
> Luke 11:23

Jesus, of course, knew who He was, and that there is no middle ground. He simply spoke the truth when He made that statement.

You may say, *That's ridiculous.* Is it really, or is it the truth? I believe the fact that you react to His name proves what He said is true. If Jesus wasn't someone, something, very significant, you wouldn't have the reaction you do. Only something, or someone, supernatural can cause such a reaction. You have never seen Jesus, you've never met Him, you may not even pay attention to Him, and yet He affects you—why? Would you be uncomfortable if I were to talk to you about Buddha? No, of course not. He has no power. He was, in fact, just a man.

None of us can ignore Jesus. No matter how much we might want to believe that He is no big deal, the truth is, He is *the* big deal. If thinking about Jesus makes you uncomfortable, it is because the spirit inside you is being faced with the Truth. Your spirit knows it, and if your internal spirit is not aligned with the Spirit of Truth, then the conflict begins, and you have an uncomfortable feeling. Your spirit is sensitive to other spirits and spiritual truth. Consider these words from James, the half-brother of Jesus, when he was writing to first-century Jewish Christians.

> You believe that there is one God. You do well.
> Even the demons believe—and tremble!
> James 2:19

Did you get that? Even demonic spirits know the truth. When you are not in agreement with the little part of God that He planted in your heart, you are a house divided. You cannot have internal peace under those conditions.

Before I chose to walk with the Lord, I would get very uncomfortable whenever someone would start talking about Him. I was aware that

I was feeling uncomfortable, and I often wondered why. I thought about that a lot, and I began to look for the answer. Having studied psychology in my undergraduate classes, I knew that if I was having an emotional reaction to something largely unknown to me, there had to be some sort of connection between me and whatever it was. I have since learned that the connection is my spirit. The unrest in my spirit was causing my discomfort. The essence of me, my spirit, was not in line with the Spirit of my Creator. The pot was denying the potter.

> Therefore God also has highly exalted Him
> and given Him the name which is above every name,
> that at the name of Jesus every knee should bow, of those
> in heaven, and of those on earth, and of those under the
> earth, and that every tongue should confess that Jesus
> Christ is Lord, to the glory of God the Father.
> Philippians 2:9-11

Deep inside me, I knew the truth about Jesus all along. I had learned it when I was quite young in Sunday school. But I had forsaken and forgotten that knowledge and had chosen to live according to my own will—big mistake. My own best thinking led me into some pretty dicey situations. I wish I had listened to Him and let Him lead me all along.

> Eye has not seen, nor ear heard,
> Nor have entered into the heart of man
> the things which God has prepared for those who love Him
> 1Corinthians 2:9

I sometimes wonder what I've missed. I wonder what you've missed if you haven't been trusting the Lord with your life. We can't go back, but we can trust Him from this point forward, and we can expect good things from Him.

Blessed be the God and Father of our Lord Jesus Christ,
who has blessed us with every spiritual blessing
in the heavenly places in Christ.
Ephesians 1:3

Jesus is always standing by to pour His blessings out on us. He just wants to know that whatever He does for us, or whatever He chooses to give us, will be well received and used wisely. When we are on board with His program, and we are praying for His will to be done in our lives, then He is confident that we will in fact be good stewards of the blessings He bestows on us. His blessings toward us will then indeed be abundant.

And the Lord said, "Who then is that faithful and wise steward,
whom his master will make ruler over his household,
Blessed is that servant whom his master will find
so doing when he comes. Truly, I say to you that
he will make him ruler over all that he has"
Luke 12:42-44

It is a shame that more of us don't realize the truth about Jesus. If we understood who He is and what that means to each of us, we'd have very different perspectives on life, other people, and our own lives. Actually, not only would our perspectives be different, but our lives would also be different. It seems impossible, but even those who came into personal contact with Jesus didn't always realize who He was. There was a woman at a well who had a conversation with Jesus. She was talking about drawing water from the well. He said to her:

If you knew the gift of God, and who it is who says
to you, 'Give Me a drink,' you would have asked Him,
and He would have given you living water
John 4:10

The woman said to Him, "I know that Messiah is coming …
When He comes, He will tell us all things."
Jesus said to her, "I who speak to you am He"
John 4:25-26

Yes, if only she knew. If only we all knew …

Occasionally, Jesus flashed His power, so that there would be no mistake about who He was when someone was speaking to Him. I really like this brief passage that recounts the moment when the soldiers came to arrest Jesus before His crucifixion. Jesus and His disciples were sitting around the fire, relaxing, when all of a sudden:

Then Judas, having received a detachment of troops,
and officers from the chief priests and Pharisees,
came there with lanterns, torches, and weapons.
Jesus therefore, knowing all things that would come upon Him,
went forward and said to them, "Whom are you seeking?"
They answered Him, "Jesus of Nazareth." Jesus said to them,
"I am He." … Now when He said to them, "I am He,"
they drew back and fell to the ground
John 18:3-7

You just got to love Jesus. Here comes a bunch of guys, armed with weapons, to arrest Him, and was He worried? Not at all—He didn't even flinch. He simply walked up to them and spoke, and they dropped. All He said was, "I am He." Three little words, but oh, what a statement. The soldiers didn't know what had hit them. Jesus had just looked them in the eye and said, "I am He." He was simply saying, "I am your God, boys, and you're going to feel my presence," and they certainly did. They were knocked off their feet by the power of the Truth.

A little while later, when He was being interrogated by Pilate, Jesus again made a bold statement:

> Pilate therefore said to Him, "Are You a king then?" Jesus answered,
> "You say rightly that I am a king. For this cause I
> was born, and for this cause I have come into the
> world, that I should bear witness to the truth"
> John 18:37

I left off the last line of His statement to make a point. Pilate didn't realize the truth, because he was not willing to accept who Jesus truly was. The same is true for the rest of us. If we choose to reject the truth of who He is, then He'll leave us in the dark as well. But if we align ourselves with Jesus, He will reveal His truth to us. Here's the rest of His statement:

> Everyone who is of the truth hears My voice
> John 18:37

On another occasion, He said this:

> I am the light of the world. He who follows Me shall
> not walk in darkness, but have the light of life
> John 8:12

Another time, Jesus and His disciples were talking, and they asked Him something:

> And the disciples came and said to Him, "Why do You speak to
> them in parables?" He answered and said to them, "... it has been
> given to you to know the mysteries of the kingdom of heaven,
> but to them it has not been given ...

I speak to them in parables, because seeing they do not see,
and hearing they do not hear, nor do they understand"
Matthew 13: 10-13

God wants to teach all of us, but He is not going to waste His time or His words if we are not sincere in wanting to learn His truth. There is a verse in Proverbs about teaching a child the truth when he's young, and even if he wanders for a while, he'll find his way back.

Train up a child in the way he should go, And
when he is old he will not depart from it
Proverbs 22:6

It took me a while to find my way back, but since I've returned and have been praying and genuinely seeking to understand the word of God, He has opened my spiritual eyes to see, for the first time in some cases, the truths that are contained in His word. I don't have any special privilege or insight. I just asked God to reveal His truth to me, and He has, and is continuing to do so. He will do the same for you if you pray and ask Him.

I've read through the entire New Testament many times, and each time I do, I see things that I hadn't noticed before. Sometimes, it's so dramatic that I wonder how I could possibly have missed whatever verse it was. I know now that it was simply a matter of God feeling that it was the right time to reveal a particular truth to me for a reason known only to Him. That's the way He works. It's fun to read the Bible. God's truth is truly new every morning. There's an old saying, "When the student is ready, the teacher will appear." That's for sure.

I'd like to share this very powerful bit of Scripture about what can happen when you seek to know the truth of God's word.

> ...the God of our Lord Jesus Christ, the Father of glory,
> may give to you the spirit of wisdom and
> revelation in the knowledge of Him,
> the eyes of your understanding being enlightened;
> that you may know what is the hope of His calling,
> what are the riches of the glory of His inheritance in the saints,
> and what is the exceeding greatness of His
> power toward us who believe,
> according to the working of His mighty power
> Ephesians 1:17-19

When we declare ourselves ready, our teacher will surely come to us.

In any discussion about the divinity of Jesus, it would seem that a discussion of His miracles would be appropriate. However, if I got started on listing and discussing each of them, I'd never finish this book. So, I will leave it to you to read about them in the Bible, if you so choose. For now, I will simply say that I believe they speak for themselves. Jesus' miracles are a pretty convincing argument for His divinity. How else could you explain Jesus' ability to perform them, if He is not divine? No other person in history has been able to do anything even close to the things He did.

I would like to point out a very important truth about Jesus' miracles. He was not a showman. He did not perform those amazing feats just to show off. He did them to teach lessons and to demonstrate who He was. He used His power to back up His words so people would know that His words were true. The key here is to realize that *all* of His words are true.

For example, Jesus gave us the bottom line when He said the following:

I am the way, the truth, and the life. No one
comes to the Father except through Me
John 14:6

In fact, it is the "mother" of all bottom lines. Without Jesus, we will not get into Heaven. It's up to you and me and everyone else to decide what we're going to do with that bottom line statement.

It just occurred to me that some readers may be saying to themselves, *Now Geoff is starting to sound like one of those narrow-minded, intolerant preachers.* That is certainly not my intention here. As I said in my introduction, this book is about the truth of God's word as contained in the Holy Bible. I'm simply passing on to you what the Bible says. I'm just the messenger. It is the absolute right and privilege of each and every person to make his or her own choice to accept and believe the word of God or not. It is certainly not up to me to tell you or anyone else what to think. I look at it this way. If I'm wrong, and the Bible is not the truth, then so what? I'm just wrong, and there is no consequence for not believing the biblical teachings. However, if you are someone who rejects the Bible and you are wrong, and the biblical teachings are true, then what? Please think about that. If the Bible is true, then when we're talking about the consequences for disbelief, we are not simply talking about ten minutes in time out. We are talking about every minute, every second of forever in absolutely unimaginable misery—Hell. Are you willing to take that chance? I would encourage you to do your own investigation of God's word and make an informed decision. Because I do believe that the Bible is true, I want to be sure that you are taking your decision, whatever it is, very seriously.

Jesus understood that He needed some indisputable evidence other than His own words to prove His Divinity. Obviously, anyone can claim anything they want to claim about themselves, and what does that prove? Realizing that fact, Jesus let His actions prove His words.

> There is another who bears witness of Me,
> If I bear witness of Myself, My witness is not true.
> and I know that the witness which He witnesses of Me is true.
> You have sent to John, and he has borne witness to the truth.
> Yet I do not receive testimony from man,
> but I say these things that you may be saved.
> But I have a greater witness than John's;
> for the works which the Father has given Me to finish
> the very works that I do bear witness of Me,
> that the Father has sent Me.
> John 5:31-36

Jesus knew that healing people in this life would be meaningless, if they didn't accept the truth about Him and make it into the next life with Him. So, He performed His miracles with the intent of proving that He was more than just a preacher/teacher/prophet.

> The works that I do in My Father's name, they bear witness of Me
> John 10:25

> And many more believed because of His own word …
> Now we believe … for we ourselves have heard and we know
> that this is indeed the Christ, the Savior of the world
> John 4:41-42

God Himself made a very clear statement about who Jesus was:

… suddenly a voice came out of the cloud, saying, "This is
My beloved Son, in whom I am well pleased. Hear Him!"
Matthew 17:5

God didn't just identify Jesus as His Son; He told us in no
uncertain terms that we are to listen to Him. God sent Jesus to
earth to be our Professor Emeritus in the college of life. Anything
we need to know to live abundant, happy lives, we can learn from
Him through His words in His textbook, the Bible.

Jesus wanted His disciples to realize that they didn't have to take
only His word on who He was. He told them that it was God who
put the understanding of the truth into their minds. Let's listen in
on part of a conversation Jesus had with His disciples.

He said to them, "But who do you say that
I am?" Simon Peter answered
and said, "You are the Christ, the Son of the living God."
Jesus answered and said to him, "Blessed are you, Simon Bar-Jonah,
for flesh and blood has not revealed this to you,
but My Father who is in heaven"
John 16:15-17

Jesus made a number of statements about His true identity.

Again the high priest asked Him, saying to Him,
"Are You the Christ, the Son of the Blessed?"
Jesus said, "I am"
Mark 14:61-62

I am the bread of life. He who comes to Me shall never
hunger, and he who believes in Me shall never thirst.
John 6:35

The Bible is full of statements that point to Jesus' divinity. In fact, Jesus is the central theme of the Bible. Look at this verse from the book of Genesis when God was busy creating everything:

> Then God said, "Let Us make man in Our
> image, according to Our likeness"
> Genesis 1:26

To whom do you suppose God was speaking? Before God created the world, there was no one around for Him to talk to—except, that is, Jesus. Recall the verse, "In the beginning ... and the Word was with God." In the beginning, there was only God and Jesus. The whole point of the Bible is to get us from where we began—Creation—to where we are going Eternity. And Jesus is the key for how we get there. I recall an old song with the line, "I'm your vehicle, baby." Well, Jesus is our vehicle.

A lot of people think they can just go about their business, try to be reasonably "good" persons and then go right on in to Heaven when they die. That just isn't true. That issue is precisely why Jesus came to earth and suffered what He suffered. He knew that without Him, we cannot get into Heaven.

I think this point is where a lot of people have a problem with Christianity. They say it is too narrow minded. They don't like a religion that sets so many rules, and that says there is only one way to get to Heaven. People tend to like the "easier" religions, the "feel good" ones, the ones that talk about peace and love and being a good person, and the "oneness of everything," and all is God and God is all, and so on. I can understand why that would be appealing. It's all very dreamy and optimistic, but there is one big problem—it is not the truth. There is no accountability in those religions. In many of the "looser," for lack of a better term, religions, everything is relative, everything is okay, and everything is true, in which case, nothing is true. As soon as you have any two things that are not in complete agreement on a particular point, then at least one of them cannot be true. Sooner or later, any way of thinking and believing that lacks accountability and a bottom line of truth will eventually be exposed as false. History is replete with false prophets, false religions, and false belief systems.

Sometimes people mistake common opinion, or belief, for truth. They think that if enough people believe a certain way, then whatever they believe must be true. For example, most of the educated world once believed the world was flat. However, despite their educated and well-intentioned beliefs, the world was, and still is, round.

We cannot, by majority, vote a truth into being. Truth is truth. We don't have to accept it, but we cannot re-write it, or invent it. Truth is what it is, now and forever.

The truth in our present discussion is that Jesus is the only way to Heaven.

And Jesus said to him, "Today salvation has come to this house
...for the Son of Man has come to seek
and to save that which was lost"
Luke 19:9-10

Nor is there salvation in any other,
for there is no other name under heaven given among men
by which we must be saved
Acts 4:12-13

If you confess with your mouth the Lord Jesus
and believe in your heart that God has raised Him from the dead,
you will be saved. For with the heart one
believes unto righteousness,
and with the mouth confession is made unto salvation
Romans 10:9-11

We who first trusted in Christ should be to the praise of His glory.
In Him you also trusted, after you heard the word of truth,
the gospel of your salvation
Ephesians 1:12-13

For God did not appoint us to wrath,
but to obtain salvation through our Lord Jesus Christ,
Who died for us, that whether we wake or sleep,
we should live together with Him
1 Thessalonians 5:9-10

… that they also may obtain the salvation,
which is in Christ Jesus with eternal glory.
2 Timothy 2:10

… that the genuineness of your faith,
being much more precious than gold that perishes,
though it is tested by fire, may be found to
praise, honor, and glory at the revelation of Jesus Christ,
whom having not seen, you love.
Though now you do not see Him, yet believing,
you rejoice with joy inexpressible and full of glory,
receiving the end of your faith—the salvation of your souls
1 Peter 1:6-9

If you're wondering why I used so many verses to make this point, the reason is simple - I'm fighting for your future. The eternal destiny of your soul and your spirit depends on whether or not you believe what you have just read. I'm hoping that if you read enough truth, you will accept it as such.

In his letter to the Colossians, Paul wrote this concerning who Jesus is, and why He came to earth:

For He has rescued us from the dominion of darkness and brought us
into the kingdom of the Son He loves,
in whom we have redemption, the forgiveness of sins.
He is the image of the invisible God, the firstborn over all creation.
For by Him all things were created: things in heaven and on earth,
visible and invisible, whether thrones or powers or rulers or authorities;
all things were created by Him and for Him.
He is before all things, and in Him all things hold together.
And He is the head of the body, the church;
He is the beginning and the firstborn from among the dead,
so that in everything He might have the supremacy.
For God was pleased to have all his fullness dwell in Him,
and through Him to reconcile to Himself all things,
whether things on earth or things in heaven,
by making peace through His blood, shed on the cross
Colossians 1:13-20 (NIV)

That passage is a pretty good summation of the who, what, and why of Jesus. As a believer, I sometimes get frustrated when people dismiss or reject the message of Jesus. But, I can also understand it. For many years, I dismissed people who tried to share the truth with me. I guess it's a lot like what we go through as parents. We try to advise and counsel our kids on various things, because we have "been there and done that," and we know what they are getting themselves into. At the same time that we want so desperately to help them by saving them from themselves, we know they are still going to go ahead and do many things their own way. It's just the way it is. We all did the same thing with our own parents. If you, dear reader, are over the age of about twenty-five or so, then you'll understand this. Remember when you were quite young, your parents seemed so wise and almost godlike to you? Then when you hit twelve or thirteen, your parents mysteriously lost their minds. They suddenly had no idea what the world was about. Then when you were about twenty-five, your parents remarkably got their minds back again—funny how that works.

That's what it's like when you begin to acquire wisdom through God's truths. And the more wisdom you acquire, the more He gives you. Then, when you look at what so many people are going through as they try to manage their lives without God, you just want to shake them and say, *You don't have to go through all that stuff. There is a better way.* But as I said earlier, we all must find our own way at our own pace. Hopefully, we will all get there eventually. Sadly, some never do. Oddly, one thing that I find very encouraging is this: for people who are fortunate enough to have some warning of their impending death (I say fortunate only from the spiritual perspective, because there is nothing otherwise fortunate about drawn-out, slow suffering, as in cancer and diseases like that), those people seem to get a sense of God and the hereafter, and they make their peace with Him and gain their salvation.

It's interesting how the things of this world are so diametrically opposed to the things of God. Most people, myself included, will say it's a blessing to die instantly, such as in a plane crash, or something immediate of that nature. If you're a believer, then yes, a quick death is a blessing. But, if you're not "with Christ", and you go suddenly and unexpectedly, then it's a disaster. According to the word of God, you don't get a second chance after the fact to accept Him and become saved. That is why Christians sometimes may seem a little annoying with the urgency of their witnessing to you. It is only because they know how much is at stake and that things can change in an instant. I'm acutely aware of that fact after my accident. I was literally a few inches or microseconds away from being splattered all over the road. It so happens that I'm saved, so I'd have been all right, but for those who aren't, death can produce a very different ending to their story.

Now let's look at the elusive third truth - Jesus is alive and He lives in and through believers so that their lives can be full and rewarding. Remember what Jesus said:

> I have come that they may have life,
> and that they may have it more abundantly.
> John 10:10

Why will we have life more abundantly? Because when we allow Jesus to live in and through us, what we are really doing is inviting His Spirit, the Holy Spirit, to live in us. Of course, Jesus can't cram His body into ours, so He sends His Spirit to live in our heart and mind. When the Holy Spirit lives in us, then we have the ultimate mind with all of His wisdom as our partner to help us in the affairs of this life. How can we go wrong if we have working within us the Spirit who knows all, sees all, and understands all? When we accept the Holy Spirit as our guide and teacher and helper, there is nothing that we can't handle. Remember this verse?

> I can do all things through Christ who strengthens me
> Philippians 4:13

The Holy Spirit is the Spirit of Jesus and the Spirit of God. When a person accepts Jesus as his or her Savior and Jesus sends His

Holy Spirit to reside inside that new Christian, that person now has unlimited intellectual and spiritual resources at his or her disposal. In the next chapter, I'll discuss the Holy Spirit in more depth as we look into His nature and His ministry.

> And when they had prayed,
> the place where they were assembled together was shaken;
> and they were all filled with the Holy Spirit,
> and they spoke the word of God with boldness
> Acts 4:31

Jesus also told the rest of us that God will give us the Holy Spirit if we will just ask Him.

> If you then ... know how to give good gifts to your children,
> how much more will your heavenly Father
> give the Holy Spirit to those who ask Him!
> Luke 11:13

When I was beginning to explore Christianity, I had questions about some things that I couldn't easily explain to myself. I tend to be inquisitive and analytical. So, of course I did what I always do. I started reading a lot and searching for answers to my questions. In the paragraphs below, I've shared some of the things that I wondered about and some of the thought processes I went through to help me get to my present state of faith in and acceptance of God's truths.

I've included these things in the hope that they may help you if you have questions, or if you're wondering about some of the same things. Or perhaps some of this might be helpful to you if you're trying to help someone else in his or her search for the truth.

Anyhow, take a look, I believe you will find the information to be thought provoking and hopefully, helpful.

Let's begin with what we know.

We know Jesus existed. There are many ancient documents other than the Bible that speak of Him. Writers who were not supporters of Jesus wrote about Him. His existence does not appear to be in question. The primary conflict with Jesus arises from what He said about Himself. Jesus was a man who claimed to be the Son of God. That's an extraordinary thing for someone to say, and it raises two obvious possibilities. Either He was telling the truth, or He was lying. Well, if you believe that He is who He said He is, then we don't need to say anything else. But if you don't believe Him, or you're not sure, then read on.

The first thing that comes to mind is all the miracles. The religious leaders of the day wanted to get rid of Jesus because He was attracting a whole lot of followers and He was challenging their position as the top dogs in the religion business. Interestingly, none of the people who opposed Him ever disputed that He performed all those miracles. In fact, that was one of the primary causes for their concern with Him. They couldn't deny that He possessed some sort of unusual, supernatural power, because they witnessed His miracles; they were on display for all to see.

It seems to me that if those miracles were just fairy tales, we would certainly have some writings somewhere by someone from Jesus' day who wrote to prove that they didn't happen. To my knowledge, no such writings exist. Therefore, I think we must accept that the miracles did in fact happen, just as we are told they did. Now, if we accept that Jesus did perform all those miracles, and since no one before or since has been able to do anything like them, how can we explain them? How did He do them? I can't offer any explanation other than what He said was true—He is Divine. Can you explain His miracles? I can't even begin to think of how someone could have done any of those things without having some supernatural, superhuman power. I personally believe that not only did He have supernatural power, but it was Godly power. All of His miracles were done to benefit people other than Himself. Knowing that He possessed unlimited power, Jesus certainly could have prevented the torture that He endured before His crucifixion, and of course, the crucifixion itself. But in what I consider to be an even greater display of power, He allowed it all to happen to Himself. Only someone with the mind of God could do that, in my opinion. If an ordinary person had access to the kind of power that Jesus possessed, it would be far too easy and tempting to abuse the power and use it for personal gain at the expense of others, unless the person holding the power was of exceptional character. Jesus was clearly not an ordinary person. His power and His behavior argue something not of this earth.

Now we come to the biggest issue regarding Jesus and his true identity—the resurrection. Again, we have two possibilities. Either Jesus did rise again, or He didn't. If He didn't, then what happened to His body? There is a lot of evidence to support the resurrection; a lot of people saw Him in His resurrected state. But if you don't believe that He rose again, then I ask you again, what happened to His body? If His opponents had taken it, they would surely have produced it as evidence, and that would have ended the whole thing right then and there. Christianity would never have begun, since it is all based on Jesus and His resurrection. So we are left with the possibility that Jesus' followers took His body. Certainly, that seems to be the most logical explanation. However, if that were true, then what followed doesn't make any sense. If Jesus' followers had stolen His body, then of course they would have known that although He was a great teacher, in the end, He died like any other man, and the deal was over. Further, if it were true that His disciples stole the body, why did they continue to very zealously promote His story and their new religion? They had absolutely nothing to gain. Instead, they had everything to lose, including their lives. There certainly was no potential for financial gain, and they didn't achieve fame or political power. In fact, they were ridiculed, persecuted, and killed because of their faith. Ten of the original twelve disciples were martyred.

So why did they continue in their fervent beliefs? Obviously, they believed completely in what they were preaching. They were absolutely convinced in the truth of Jesus and His teachings and His identity. But why? For one thing, a lot of them had seen and even physically touched Jesus after His resurrection. At that point, there was no longer any question or doubt about Jesus' words and the truth of who He is. Here's an interesting little aside. You've heard the term "doubting Thomas"? If you don't know, it originated with one of the disciples—Thomas. After Jesus had risen, Thomas hadn't yet seen Him, and when he was told that Jesus was indeed alive, he didn't believe it.

After His resurrection, Jesus in His supernatural, eternal body was able to suddenly appear and disappear like people do in fantasy movies. But Jesus did it in real life. John wrote about Jesus' removal of Thomas' doubts. The disciples were in a room, behind closed doors when Jesus suddenly appeared.

> Now Thomas … one of the twelve, was
> not with them when Jesus came.
> The other disciples therefore said to him,
> "We have seen the Lord." So he said to them,
> "Unless I see in His hands the print of the nails, and put my
> finger into the print of the nails, and put my hand into His side,
> I will not believe." And after eight days His disciples were again
> inside, and Thomas with them. Jesus came, the doors being shut,

and stood in the midst, and said, "Peace to you!" Then He said
to Thomas, "Reach your finger here, and look at My hands;
and reach your hand here, and put it into My side.
Do not be unbelieving, but believing."
And Thomas answered and said to Him,
"My Lord and my God!"
Jesus said to him, "Thomas, because you
have seen Me, you have believed.
Blessed are those who have not seen and yet have believed."
And truly Jesus did many other signs in
the presence of His disciples,
which are not written in this book; but these
are written that you may believe
that Jesus is the Christ, the Son of God,
and that believing you may have life in His name
John 20:24-31

Jesus appeared to the disciples and numerous other people on
several other occasions as well. Each time, it was to demonstrate to
them His true nature, and to assure them that they would be just
fine without Him. He told them what they were to do from that
point forward.

Jesus came and spoke to them, saying, "All authority
has been given to Me in heaven and on earth. Go
therefore and make disciples of all the nations,
baptizing them in the name of the Father and of
the Son and of the Holy Spirit, teaching them to
observe all things that I have commanded you; and
lo, I am with you always, to the end of the age"
Matthew 28:18-20

Jesus did many things after His resurrection that were not specifically recorded in the Bible but which I am sure were done with great purpose and intent to supercharge the faith of His disciples. Those men were going to need unshakable faith to carry on the ministry that had been given them, especially in the face of such severe opposition. John, one of Jesus' inner three, ended his Gospel with this:

And there are also many other things that Jesus did,
which if they were written one by one, I suppose
that even the world itself could not contain
the books that would be written
John 21:25

The disciples knew the truth about who Jesus was, because they had seen Him after He had risen. Remember, He had told them that He would be killed, and that on the third day He would rise again, and He did! And later they experienced the Day of Pentecost when the Holy Spirit came and filled the believers, also just as Jesus had said it would happen.

And He said to them …
"you shall receive power when the Holy Spirit has come upon you;
and you shall be witnesses to Me … to the end of the earth"
Acts 1:7-8

Jesus had proved Himself as someone who speaks the truth because He had said He would do many of the things He did before He actually did them. And please realize, some of the things He said He would do were a bit out of the ordinary, to say the least. Remember, He said He was going to wake up Lazarus, who had been dead for four days, and bring him back to life. That's a pretty bold statement for Jesus to have made unless He was awfully sure of Himself. The question I have for you is—are you sure of Him?

When I think about His resurrection and the fact He said on several occasions that it would happen, and then it did happen, it becomes impossible, at least for me, to deny that He is exactly who He said He is—the Divine Son of God. And with that in mind then, it seems absurd for me to doubt anything else that He said. I've chosen to believe Jesus and what He said, and what He continues to say to me. That is my personal choice. It's up to you to make your own choice. If you are still unsure at this point, I hope that at the very least, you will take a long, hard look at Him. The possibilities for your life as a follower of Jesus are endless and exciting.

I'd like to leave you with a simple prayer. If you've already accepted Jesus as your personal Savior, then this is just repetition. If, however, you have not accepted Him, then this prayer can be the beginning of your new life in Christ. Welcome to eternity in paradise!

"Dear Jesus, I know I'm a sinner and I've fallen short in many ways. I am sorry for the things I've done. I ask You now to forgive me for all I've done that is displeasing to You. I need You in my life to help me and guide me. I do believe You died for me to cleanse me of my sins so that I can be acceptable to the Father. Jesus, I surrender my life to You. Please come into my heart and teach me Your ways and lead me in my life. I want to change from who I am and become the person You created me to be. Thank you for loving me and for saving me. Your child ... (your name)"

†

THE HOLY SPIRIT

Our Helper

... the fruit of the Spirit is love, joy, peace, longsuffering, kindness, goodness, faithfulness, gentleness, self-control

Galations 5:22-23

The Holy Spirit: Who is He? Why is He important? What does He mean to you and me? What does He do?

In this chapter, you will find the answers to all of those questions.

Who is the Holy Spirit? He is the Spirit of God, and the Spirit of Jesus. The Holy Spirit is in effect God's agent. He is the entity that comes to live within you when you accept Jesus as your personal Savior. He becomes that "still, small voice" that speaks to you when you are faced with certain situations or decisions or opportunities (both for good and for bad). The Holy Spirit is the voice of God speaking to you from within you. He is your companion, your guide, your helper, and your conscience. He is the one who enables you to live a godly life. You don't have it in you (none of us do) to live a godly life unless you have the Holy Spirit living within you.

When we surrender ourselves to Jesus, the Holy Spirit comes to live in us, and it is He who lives from that point on, not we ourselves. We become dead to sin and alive in Christ when we accept Jesus and His Holy Spirit into our lives.

Jesus told His disciples that He would send the Holy Spirit to them to help them spread the gospel after He was gone, and it happened just as He said it would.

> And when they had prayed, the place where they were assembled together was shaken; and they were all filled with the Holy Spirit, and they spoke the word of God with boldness
>
> Acts 4:31

Jesus also told the rest of us that God will give us the Holy Spirit if we will just ask Him.

> If you then ... know how to give good gifts to your children, how much more will your heavenly Father give the Holy Spirit to those who ask Him!
>
> Luke 11:13

The very Spirit of our God wants to live within each of us to help us in our lives. How can we lose, and why would we refuse? I know I'm repeating myself, but the more I research and write, the more my love for Jesus grows as I realize who He is and what He has given me and done for me. Near as I can tell, there is no limit to His love for me. And of course, there is no limit to His love for you. His love is not conditional. We can't win it or lose it by our performance. He loves us freely, unconditionally, and completely. We simply need to accept Him at His word and bask in the light and warmth of God's pure love as given to us through and by His Son Jesus Christ. Then we can allow Him to live in and through us by His Holy Spirit.

... God demonstrates His own love toward us, in that
while we were still sinners, Christ died for us.
Romans 5:8

We don't have to be clean and pure before God will love and accept us. First of all, it's impossible. We are not now and will never be good enough. God knows that, and yet He loves us anyhow. He just wants us to accept His love, trust in His love, and love Him back. He will work on the task of cleaning us up. Personally, I love it when I hear the voice of the Holy Spirit saying to me, "Geoff, do you really want to do that? Are you sure about that? You know you shouldn't be doing that." I don't take that as, "Oh no, here He goes again getting on my case." Instead, I say, "Thank you, Lord, for loving me and keeping an eye on me."

I accept His guidance as an assurance of His love and concern for me and my well-being. As a child, don't you remember times when you felt loved when your parent disciplined you for something? You knew deep inside that they did it because they loved you and were training you up in the way you should go. That's what the Holy Spirit does when He is living inside you. Talk about a moral compass—when you are being led by the Holy Spirit, you cannot go wrong.

For a while, I was involved in operating an after-school care and summer camp program. I can remember times when some of the children would seem to bond closer to the owner of the business when she would chastise them for something. I knew immediately that they sensed she cared about them. It was sad because I also had firsthand knowledge that some of those same children did not get that affirmation of love from their own parents. Those children so desperately wanted to feel loved by someone. That is why it is so very critical that you align yourself with the Holy Spirit. If you're searching for love and you are not secure in God's love, then you will as the old song says, go "looking for love in all the wrong places."

We all need the kind of care and love that we receive from the Holy Spirit. He loves us and wants only the best for us. If we will allow Him, He will care for us and protect us from ourselves and our human desires and impulses that could otherwise lead us into trouble, possibly serious trouble.

When you have the Holy Spirit as your guide and companion, you have within you the ultimate big brother, the ultimate parental figure, the ultimate friend. Life is amazing when you walk with the Holy Spirit. Even simple things such as what you should say in a given situation can be handled for you by Him. I'm sure you've heard someone say this next phrase or perhaps you've said it yourself when you've been in an exasperating situation, "Lord, give me strength." The speaker may not have realized it at the time, but if he or she had the Holy Spirit within him or her, he or she could have asked Him, and He would have indeed given the strength, the words, or whatever was appropriate for the moment. Jesus, said to His disciples:

> Do not worry beforehand, or premeditate what you will
> speak. But whatever is given you in that hour, speak
> that; for it is not you who speak, but the Holy Spirit
> Mark 13:11

If that strikes you as being a little "out there" or a little supernatural, it's because it is. The realm of God and Godly concepts, and His whole operation for that matter, is out of this world. This world is Satan's realm. God put us here to see if we'll pass the test and gain entrance into His kingdom. You can greatly enhance your chances of success by asking the Holy Spirit to come and live in your heart. When He is running your show, you are much less likely to get into trouble. Please note that I said you are less likely. I didn't say you won't get yourself into trouble at all. Even with the Holy Spirit living within you, you will still retain your free will. If you want to sin or do something that you know you shouldn't, you are free to do so. What the Spirit does for you is speak to you in His gentle reminding way to point out your choices at the moment and to ask you if you're sure that you want to proceed in whatever direction you may be contemplating. If your heart's desire is to do God's will, then the slight nudge from the Spirit is usually sufficient to keep you in line. But as always, the choice is yours.

When you start to stray from the appointed course, you will feel a check in your spirit. That's when you know the Holy Spirit is doing His job in you. I'm smiling again as I'm writing this section. I just love it when I think of God loving me enough to mind every step I take. When I'm not sure about something, I just stop and ask Him what He thinks I should do or say, and the Holy Spirit speaks to me with His answer. How awesome is that? The Spirit of Almighty God takes the time to watch over me every second of the day. He will do the same for you if you just ask Him.

> Now we have received, not the spirit of the world, but
> the Spirit who is from God, that we might know the
> things that have been freely given to us by God
> 1 Corinthians 2:12

I want to give you a recent example from my own life about how the Holy Spirit moves in our lives to teach us things that we need to learn, *when* we need to learn them. Or perhaps I should say when we are *ready* to learn them.

One of the things I sometimes struggle with is impatience with and intolerance of people. Usually I'm able to say *Geoff, you're being a jerk by thinking this or that about this guy.* But on this occasion, I couldn't seem to get my mind under control. It occurred over two evenings while I was enjoying my nightly workout at the YMCA. I was on the elliptical machine, which I usually "ride" for thirty minutes, and a guy was on the one next to me riding it rather vigorously. He was making some fairly loud and distinct breathing sounds—annoying breathing sounds to be exact. It was like the sound you hear when you take your fingernail and let some air out of the valve stem on a car tire. This was going on over and over, in and out for about twenty minutes. I looked over and saw that he had his mouth closed. I thought, *Look, you jerk, open your darn mouth and breathe through it and then I won't have to listen to this irritating sound all night!* I just wanted to slap him. I wondered if he was from some nose-breathing cult or something. I was working myself into a ridiculous snit. I couldn't decide if I was madder at him or me—him for making the noise, or me for letting it bother me.

I looked over at the timer on his machine, and I noticed his time was going to run out about four minutes before mine. So then I just tried to concentrate on the fact that if I could hang on, I would have four minutes of peaceful "ellipticalling" at the end of my ride. His time did run out and I thought, *Finally, that madness is over. Now I can relax and enjoy my workout.* Of course the only madness was all mine, but that's for another story.

Well, the next night, I got on the elliptical machine and was happily pedaling along when guess who steps onto the machine next to me? You got it—Captain Nose-Breathe. I thought to myself, *Are you kidding me? What have I done to deserve this?* No, I didn't really want God to answer that one. As you can imagine, I was really miserable this time because since I had started before the Captain, I knew that my time would end before his and therefore the noise would be continuing throughout my entire ride, which still had about twenty-five minutes to go. I was certain that my brain would explode by then. After all, how could anybody be expected to endure such an annoyance? Fortunately, God had evidently decided that my brain exploding would place an unnecessarily messy burden on the custodial staff, so He had the Captain shorten his workout. After only about fifteen minutes, he got off the machine, much to my delight, and walked over to the moist towelette dispenser to get a towelette to come back and wipe off the machine. When he was returning, I had the first opportunity to see him head-on. He had a tracheotomy. At that moment, my brain almost did explode—inward. I felt less than an inch tall. I had been mentally criticizing and insulting a man who has a very serious condition. I don't know for a fact, but I suspect he lost his larynx to cancer. As I'm writing this, my eyes are tearing up. I cannot believe I could have had such thoughts about a man who may well have been in the gym fighting for his life. I have since spent time in prayer asking God for forgiveness for my careless, unfair, and selfish thoughts about a fellow human being, whom I had no right to criticize, and for whom my criticism was absurdly inaccurate.

I wish I could speak to that man, but I've not seen him since those two evenings. Sometimes I wonder if his presence next to me was ordained by God to teach me a huge lesson. As I stated in an earlier chapter, we truly do not know the battles that others are fighting. We must learn to have compassion and understanding for our fellow man at all times. I think we would find that more often than not, when someone says or does something that annoys us, our annoyance is only a reflection of our own state of mind at the time. If we were truly happy and involved in our own life-moments, we probably wouldn't even notice most of the things other people are doing. We would be more likely to live and let live.

Since that episode, I have prayed for that man, and I have thanked God that I have not had to fight that particular battle.

Like everyone, I all too frequently forget how truly blessed I am. Someone once asked me, "Geoff, can you think of anyone else whose problems you would like to exchange for yours?" I thought about that for awhile and then I realized no, I wouldn't want anyone else's troubles. Mine really aren't that bad when I consider them in the grand scheme of things. Thank you, Lord, for my problems. I can handle them.

You may be wondering what this has to do with the Holy Spirit. Everything! It is the Holy Spirit who speaks the words of God to our hearts and minds. I believe that God had chosen that moment in time to teach me an important lesson about compassion and understanding. He wanted to be sure I understood the error in my thinking about the judging of others, especially since I am unqualified and have no right to judge anyone at any time. It was the Holy Spirit who was working in my heart and mind by convicting me of my unfair, inappropriate, and selfish feelings and thoughts.

Here is a more dramatic episode in which the Holy Spirit intervened in my life - in fact He saved my life. Several years ago, I was walking into a waterfront condo building that was under construction. They were laying blocks on the fifth floor. As I was about to walk into the ground level parking garage, suddenly a loud voice rang out inside my head. "Stop Now!!" It was so loud and so emphatic that I just froze. Then immediately, about three feet in front of me, several cinder blocks smashed on the ground. It scared the heck out of me. I looked up and saw some pretty nervous men looking down from the fifth floor. They knew what had almost happened. If I had taken one more step, I would have been crushed under those blocks. How do I know it was the Holy Spirit? I just do. The voice inside my head knew exactly what to say and how to say it to get me to stop at that precise instant. If I had hesitated in my reaction at all, I would be dead. There was only a fraction of a second between the voice and the crash. As it was, I was hit by fragments of the blocks as they shattered in front of me. I was that close.

My point is this. You can believe in the Holy Spirit and you can trust Him completely. He is there to take care of you. Allow Him to do His job in your life. You will be better for it. I've thought about that incident many times and wondered why I wasn't killed. The only thing I can think of is that the Holy Spirit knew one day the Father would call on me to write about His truth; the Holy Spirit had to keep me from harm until that time. A weird thought just crossed my mind (it happens frequently). Now that the book is finished, am I still safe? We'll see, I guess.

Once Jesus, the human, left this planet, all communication from God to man has been via the Holy Spirit. As Jesus was nearing the end of His time here, He said this to His disciples:

> But the Helper, the Holy Spirit, whom the
> Father will send in My name,
> He will teach you all things
> John 14:26

Jesus was preparing them for what would be happening after He was gone. They couldn't grasp it all at the time, but they soon understood the truth about this man they had grown to love. I know we're taught not to envy, but don't you wish you could have been one of those guys and spent three years with Jesus, or even three minutes? It had to be amazing to be in His presence. One day we'll know what it's like, but for now we must just love Him and trust in His word as delivered to us by His Holy Spirit.

He did not leave us alone and empty-handed. We have at our "fingertips" the Spirit of God, with all His wisdom and knowledge, if we will simply humble ourselves and receive His awesome gift to us. All we need to do is ask. It is that simple.

> Then Peter said to them,
> "Repent, and let every one of you be baptized in the
> name of Jesus Christ for the remission of sins; and
> you shall receive the gift of the Holy Spirit"
> Acts 2:38

The gift of the Spirit is not restricted to those to whom Peter was actually speaking. It is available to all of us right now if we choose to accept Him.

In this book, I talk about a lot of things. If you are not a seasoned veteran of Christianity or a student of the word, or simply used to thinking in godly terms, then much of what I discuss with you may be a bit confusing. That's okay, it certainly was confusing to me at first, and sometimes still is confusing. That's quite natural, actually. In fact, the Bible refers to the mystery of faith. Godly concepts are way beyond us. It takes time for us to grow into them. That is where the Holy Spirit comes in. He helps to open the eyes of our understanding, and He opens our hearts to receive His truth.

> The natural man does not receive the things of the Spirit of God,
> for they are foolishness to him;
> nor can he know them, because they are spiritually discerned
> 1 Corinthians 2:13-14

> And He opened their understanding, that they
> might comprehend the Scriptures
> Luke 24:25

> … the God of our Lord Jesus Christ, the Father of glory,
> may give to you the spirit of wisdom and
> revelation in the knowledge of Him,
> the eyes of your understanding being enlightened; that you may
> know …what is the exceeding greatness of His power toward us
> who believe, according to the working of His mighty power.
> Ephesians 1:17-19

I wish I had gained a greater understanding of the Holy Spirit a lot sooner. I had always thought of Him as a sort of stepchild of God. I didn't realize that He is so important. Actually, He is so very important to God and Jesus, that Jesus Himself said this:

> Therefore I say to you, every sin and blasphemy will be forgiven
> men, but the blasphemy against the Spirit will not be forgiven
> men. Anyone who speaks a word against the Son of Man, it will
> be forgiven him; but whoever speaks against the Holy Spirit, it
> will not be forgiven him, either in this age or in the age to come
> Matthew 12: 31-32

Whoa! Those are very strong words. Do you realize what Jesus was saying just then? There is one particular sin, of the billions of sins that we could commit, that will not be forgiven. Jesus said we can even speak badly of Him, but not of His Spirit. That's interesting. In fact, I wasn't at all sure I understood it, so I went to a commentary to look for help. What I found was that Jesus, being a man, could accept men's criticism of Him, but He could not and would not accept criticism of His Spirit, the essence of God. That makes sense. Think of it this way. We will often accept criticism of ourselves, but if someone criticizes our spouse or our children or parents, well, them's fightin' words. You can mess with me, but don't mess with those I love.

Jesus loves the Holy Spirit. The Spirit is the extension of God, the Father, and the source of Jesus' power. So, if you've ever wondered if you've sinned to the point where God cannot forgive you, if you haven't blasphemed the Holy Spirit, then no, you have not sinned too much for forgiveness. I don't even want to think about committing the unforgivable sin. Where would I go for help if I can't be forgiven by God? There is nowhere to go. I cannot imagine such a feeling of complete hopelessness and despair. So please, dear reader, don't ever insult God's Spirit. I want to be able to meet you one day in Heaven.

In my investigation of the Holy Spirit, I learned that He has been part of God's program from the very beginning. He didn't just come onto the scene on the day of Pentecost. (I don't want to get sidetracked right now, so if you want to learn more about the Holy Spirit and Pentecost, read the book of Acts. It's the fifth book of the New Testament right after the four Gospels.)

The Holy Spirit was with God during the creation of the world.

> In the beginning God created the heavens and the earth.
> The earth was without form, and void; and
> darkness was on the face of the deep.
> And the Spirit of God was hovering over the face of the waters
> Genesis1:1-2

The Holy Spirit is the one who inspired all the biblical writers from Moses, the writer of Genesis, right on through John and his book of Revelation. Timothy told us of God's inspiriation of Scripture.

All Scripture is given by inspiration of God,
and is profitable for doctrine, for reproof, for
correction, for instruction in righteousness,
2 Timothy 3:16

The Holy Spirit has been quite busy over the years. He didn't just inspire and teach, He also helped in the creation of Jesus the human. He was the one who set Mary with child, in the absence of a human father of Jesus.

Now the birth of Jesus Christ was as follows:
After His mother Mary was betrothed to Joseph,
before they came together, she was found
with child of the Holy Spirit.
Matthew 1:18

What does the Holy Spirit mean to us? What the Holy Spirit means to us is that with His help, we can begin to live lives that will be pleasing to our Lord and Creator—Jesus. By ourselves, we cannot begin to approach any reasonable degree of godliness. Our natural, sinful nature precludes that possibility. We simply cannot live godly, Christian lives through any means of our own. There was only one person who could live a Christian life—Christ Himself.

So then, what do we do? Just as with any other problem for which we don't have a self-available solution, we ask for help. Only this time, we get the ultimate source of help—the Helper Himself, the Holy Spirit of God. Since we cannot, on our own, live as God would have us live, the Holy Spirit comes to live inside us and guide us in godly living. Jesus himself cannot live in us; there's only room for one body at a time in each of us.

But His Spirit fits into us quite nicely. Paul talked about Christ
living in us.

> I have been crucified with Christ;
> it is no longer I who live, but Christ lives in me;
> and the life which I now live in the flesh I
> live by faith in the Son of God,
> who loved me and gave Himself for me
> Galatians 2:20

That's an interesting passage. I'd like to look at it more closely.
Obviously, when Paul wrote: "I have been crucified with Christ," he
didn't mean he was actually killed. He wouldn't have been able to
write those words. He was referring to the fact that his old, sinful
nature was dead. He gave it up when he accepted Christ, and now
he is a new creation—a forgiven, sanctified child of God. Therefore,
it was no longer the old Paul living his old sinful life; he was the new
and improved Paul who was living his new, transformed life in which
Jesus, through His Holy Spirit, was guiding his steps. What's cool
about all this is that you and I and everyone else can have the same
experience—a life in which the Holy Spirit guides us. I cannot think
of any other mind that I would rather have running my show than
the mind of my loving heavenly Father—God Himself. So, as Paul
said, the life he was now living was being led by the Holy Spirit, the
ultimate, unerring tour guide.

> It is the Spirit who gives life; the flesh profits nothing.
> The words that I speak to you are spirit, and they are life
> John 6:63

Speaking of life, let's talk for a moment about yours. Which life
are you now living—the old one or the new one? "Geoff, what do
you mean?" I'm talking about the phrase that you've heard many

times, but may not have understood. I'm talking about being "born again." Uh oh, here comes that weirdo Christian stuff. Hold on a moment, dear reader. If that phrase has never been explained to you, please allow me to explain it.

> Jesus answered and said to him, "Most assuredly, I say to you, unless one is born again, he cannot see the kingdom of God."
> John 3:3

> Most assuredly, I say to you, unless one
> is born of water and the Spirit,
> he cannot enter the kingdom of God.
> That which is born of the flesh is flesh,
> and that which is born of the Spirit is spirit.
> John 3:5-6

What was Jesus talking about when He said one must be born again? He did not mean a second physical birth. He was referring to a spiritual re-birth. When we are born the first time as a baby human, we are alive physically, but dead spiritually. That is because of the separation from God that we all experienced when Adam sinned by eating from the forbidden tree. From that point forward, all mankind has been born into the sinful human race. To restore our own personal relationship with God, we must each make a conscious decision to accept Jesus as our personal Lord and Savior. No one can do that for us. There is no surrogacy here. If you confess your sins to Jesus, ask for His forgiveness, surrender your life to Him, and ask Him into your heart, then the Holy Spirit will come to live in you and you will be spiritually re-born—thus, born again. You will still be you, with all your personality and memories intact. But you will have a new spirit nature. If you were sincere in your desire to turn your life over to Jesus, then His Spirit living in you will begin to work on your heart and mind. You will find some of your thoughts and desires changing—all for the better, I can assure you. Living with and for the Lord is truly living. You may have thought you've been living all right up to this point, but once you're born again, you really start to live for the first time in your life.

For some people, the transformation happens gradually. For others, it's pretty quick. But for everyone, it is supernatural and wonderful. When the love of God is operating inside you, you start learning how powerful love can be in so many ways. In the next chapter, I'll give you God's description of love. When you read it, you will see how deeply, richly, and sincerely you will be able to love others in your life. Love is the fuel for our lives. When we have the love of God in us, we experience life and love in ways we couldn't have imagined before. Remember, that's what God wants for us. He made us to be loving beings. That is why He gave us His Holy Spirit to live and love through us. Imagine the impact you can have on those you care about when you start loving them with the love of God. That is when you will truly "let your light shine" on others.

> The love of God has been poured out in our hearts
> by the Holy Spirit who was given to us.
> Romans 5:5

Isn't that amazing? One of the primary purposes God had in mind when He gave us the Holy Spirit was to enable us to love more. Try to imagine for just a moment what this world would be like if everyone had the love of God operating in them by the power of the Holy Spirit. Of course, that will not happen, but you know what? You can surround yourself with that kind of love in your own inner circle of family and friends. When you become born again and begin to radiate God's love to your loved ones, they will pick up on it, and one by one, they will want what you have. Eventually you may see that most, if not all of them, will accept the Lord, and then your family will be an incredible group of deeply loving people who enrich each other's lives as never before. It's something to think about and strive toward. Don't be surprised when it happens. When the Holy Spirit gets down to business, lives are changed and love abounds.

Here is a question for you. Have you ever wondered why for the most part, Christians don't smoke or drink? Or if they do drink, they keep it in moderation. Part of the reason, especially with drinking, is that when people drink to excess, they tend to do and or say things they wouldn't do or say if they were sober, some of which can be quite dangerous or harmful to themselves, others, and relationships. That in itself is a good reason to take it easy on the drinking.

However, the biggest reason for none or limited drinking is largely unknown outside the Christian world.

Do you not know that your body is the temple
of the Holy Spirit who is in you, whom you have
from God, and you are not your own?
1Corinthians 6:19

That is a very sobering verse (no pun intended). When you invite the Holy Spirit to live in you, you become His home. That changes things, doesn't it? If the Spirit of God is living in you, what kind of house keeper are you going to be? When friends or family come over, don't you clean up your house? Well in what condition do you want the home of the Holy Spirit to be? Do you think He would be pleased to be in a sloppy, smoke-filled, drunken house? I realize this is a pretty strong concept to grasp and accept, but it is true. If you want the help and blessings of the Spirit of God, why would you show Him any less courtesy and respect than you would show any of your human guests? That's something to think about.

One of the things I formerly struggled with was my language. I never had what I would call an extremely foul mouth, but my language was bad enough. When I first found the Lord, my speech didn't clean up much, and I wondered why not. I prayed about it, because when I said certain things, I felt a check in my spirit, so I knew there was an internal conflict going on. But I didn't know how to overcome it. Then one day as I was reading, I came across this next verse.

> Let no corrupt word proceed out of your mouth,
> but what is good for necessary edification, that
> it may impart grace to the hearers.
> And do not grieve the Holy Spirit of God,
> by whom you were sealed for the day of redemption.
> Let all bitterness, wrath, anger, clamor, and
> evil speaking be put away from you …
> Ephesians 4:29-31

Reading that verse gave me one of those "right between the eyes" moments. By my careless, inappropriate speech, I was grieving the Holy Spirit. Yes, that Holy Spirit. The one who had so richly blessed me with His love and grace—the one who had transformed my life as He renewed my mind. I had gratefully accepted all His gifts and blessings, and yet I was insulting and grieving Him. Dear reader, when you allow the Lord and His Spirit into your life and let them surround you with their love and blessings, you will understand what I'm saying right now. You will never want to hurt Them or "grieve" Them, not any more than you would want to insult or grieve your mother or your spouse or anyone you love.

Sometimes it seems as though portions of this book are my confessions. Perhaps they are. I certainly have enough to confess in my life, as we all do. Maybe my words will touch a nerve in you and help you to see that it's okay to trust in the Lord and share your secrets with Him. Don't worry, He already knows them all, but He wants to hear you admit them. In so doing, you will set yourself free of them. He is just waiting for you to come to Him and lay them all at His feet. Then He will say to you as He said to the woman, "Your sins are forgiven you. Go and sin no more."

Confession is the catharsis that finally and forever grants us true freedom and peace. A woman who holds a special place in my heart has a saying that fits right here. She says "You're only as sick as your secrets." If she is correct, and I believe she is, then when you offer your secrets up to Jesus, you also hand Him your sickness. It's no longer yours, it's His, and He can handle it and heal it once and for all. Where that tormenting secret once resided, the Holy Spirit fills the void with His love and grace. The guilt and self-recriminations are gone, and the love of God grows within you. Only Christ and His Holy Spirit can grant that kind of healing. Remember what Paul said:

> I have been crucified with Christ; it is no longer I who live,
> but Christ lives in me
> Galatians 2:20

When Christ, through His Holy Spirit, lives in you, you will for the first time in your life be truly alive—alive as though you've never known life before. Yes, you'll still have your ups and downs and arounds and maybe even some upside-downs, but you will find your life to be so very much worth the living. You will know where you're going and how to get there. And as you are going, the journey will be meaningful. What the Lord has planned for your life is unknown to you or me, but you can trust that He will give you the desires of your heart if you trust Him and follow Him.

Jesus gave us this assurance:

For your heavenly Father knows that you need all these things.
But seek first the kingdom of God and His righteousness,
and all these things shall be added to you
Matthew 6:32-33

The Holy Spirit will be the best friend you've ever known. No human can love you as He does. No human can offer you such perfect, unerring guidance. And no human can bring healing to your wounded heart as can the Holy Spirit. Trust in the Holy Spirit; invite Him into your life and your heart. In so doing, you will experience the joyous re-birth of your soul into the newness of life that only Jesus and His Holy Spirit can offer.

But when the kindness and the love of God our Savior toward man appeared, not by works of righteousness which we have done, but according to His mercy He saved us, through the washing of regeneration and renewing of the Holy Spirit, whom He poured out on us abundantly through Jesus Christ our Savior
Titus 3:4-6

✝

LOVE

The Greatest of These

L ove. Four little letters, but it is one of the most important words in the world. It conjures feelings of the sweetness of a kiss, and the agony of lost love, of ecstatic bliss, and of unbearable hurt, of the best and worst moments of your life. Nothing can bring such happiness or such pain as can love. Fortunes have been spent, wars have been fought, lives have been taken, lives have been spared, and lives have been given, all in the name of love. Is there anything we won't do or give to obtain love? Why is that so? Why do we desire love so intensely? I believe it is because love is at the very core of our being. You and I, and everyone, were created out of love, by love, and through love.

Any serious discussion of love must begin with this next verse, which is probably the most-quoted verse in the Bible. It's the one you always see on placards in the seats at a sporting event—John 3:16. You don't as often hear verse that follows, but it completes the message of the first verse. These two verses speak of the greatest act of love in known history. It tells of the actions of a Father and a Son that were performed solely for the benefit of you and me and the entirety of humanity. Because of what this Father and Son team did, we can enjoy the incredible, undeserved blessing of eternal life in paradise.

> For God so loved the world that He gave His only begotten Son,
> that whoever believes in Him should not
> perish but have everlasting life
> John 3:16

Here is the second part of that verse.

> For God did not send His Son into the
> world to condemn the world,
> but that the world through Him might be saved
> John 3:17

That is how God expressed His love for us, all of us—the best of us and the worst of us. He loved us enough to send His only Son to be a sacrifice to save us. We were bought at a premium price—the precious blood of the Son of our God, Jesus Christ. We are so important to God that no less of a price would suffice. God offered up His very best to purchase us. With that in mind, it makes my heart hurt when I hear how people speak of God and abuse His name and insult Him. If only they knew the truth of God's love for them …

> But God demonstrates His own love toward
> us, in that while we were still sinners,
> Christ died for us. Much more then, having now been
> justified by His blood, we shall be saved from wrath through
> Him. For if when we were enemies we were reconciled to
> God through the death of His Son, much more, having
> been reconciled, we shall be saved by His life.
> Romans 5:8-10

Jesus loved us enough to submit to His Father's will and endure the miserable agony that He suffered on the cross. He did what He did just to save you and me. God offered His Son, and Jesus offered Himself. We are completely unworthy of their love and their efforts and sacrifices on our behalf, but they did it anyways. If you ever wonder what love is, or what it means, or how limitless it might be, look to the examples of God and His Son Jesus. They set the standard for love.

In the letter known as 1John, the man who walked with Jesus wrote these words to us:

> Beloved, let us love one another, for love is of God;
> and everyone who loves is born of God and knows God
> … for God is love.
> 1John 4:7-8

God is Love. Try and comprehend that revealing statement of truth. God is love. Now think about the fact that God created all of creation. That means then, that love is the driving force behind everything that exists. We exist; therefore, we have within us the very nature of God, the nature of love. Actually, that makes sense because like begets like. Since God is love, and we are born of Him, we are by nature, then, loving beings. As such, we have the capacity for loving intensely and unconditionally. When we allow ourselves to express our love nature, we become powerful beings who can bring joy and happiness to others. The love that flows from us can be life changing for someone in need. When we extend ourselves to others and let the power of God's love flow from us into them, we become conduits of healing energy to wounded hearts.

Love is the strongest force in the universe. Where love is present, evil cannot exist. Love cannot be defeated. Love is supreme. The apostle Paul wrote about the power of love.

For I am persuaded that neither death nor life,
nor angels nor principalities nor powers,
nor things present nor things to come,
nor height nor depth, nor any other created thing,
shall be able to separate us from the love of God
which is in Christ Jesus our Lord.
Romans 8:38-39

But what is love? What is the nature of love? We've been told love is a feeling, love is an emotion, love is a choice. How then can we define it? I can't. But, I'll give you the best description of love that is known to me. The words were inspired by the Author and Creator of love, God Himself.

Love is patient, love is kind.
It does not envy, it does not boast, it is not proud.
It is not self seeking, it is not easily angered,
it keeps no record of wrong doings.
Love does not delight in evil, but rejoices with the truth.
It always protects, always trusts, always
hopes, always perseveres.
LOVE NEVER FAILS.
1Corinthians 13:4-8 (NIV)

Each phrase of this passage is pregnant with truth and wisdom. As you consider the words that God used to describe love, it becomes easy to imagine that most of life's problems and conflicts would be eliminated if everyone lived as though those words were their personal code of conduct.

As he began his chapter on love, the apostle Paul wrote the following:

"And though I have the gift of prophecy,
and understand all mysteries and all knowledge,
and though I have all faith, so that I could move mountains,
but have not love, I am nothing."
1Corinthians 13:2

Paul understood that without love, we are dead. Our bodies may be alive, but our soul and spirit are lifeless. Love is the life source of our spirit, the energy of our soul. Without love, we are disconnected from our power source. We may exist and function, but we lack meaning, direction, and purpose.

To me, love has this meaning for us: *Love is the fullness and expression of the heart of God. Love is the tie that binds us all together—man and man, man and God.* All of the above considered, it is clear to me that

love is the key!

The key to what?

Love is the key to living a life of happiness, peace, fulfillment, and joy—the life that God intended for each of us to live.

Why then?

If love is so wonderful, why do so many people struggle with it? I believe it's because people have moved away from the truth of love. They've made love into something it is not. In the words above, we saw what love is. Perhaps we can begin to understand some of our problems with love when we look at what love is not.

Love is not lust. Love is not sex. Love is not a conditional bargaining chip. Love is not being in love. Love is not a guarantee of happiness (although it's certainly a step in the right direction).

As is true with any good thing, when misused, mistreated, or misunderstood, love can cause as many problems as it solves. We must respect love and not take it for granted or consider it an entitlement. Love is a precious gift that is to be honored and treasured. Love must be guarded with our lives, for our lives depend on love.

I believe there is another very important issue related to love, or I should say, the lack thereof. This particular issue involves people's inability to love and trust God. In my experience, and in the experience of many other authors who've commented on the subject, someone's distrust of God relates directly to his or her distrust of their earthly father. In short, if one didn't receive love from, or have a good, trusting relationship with their biological father, then one finds it very difficult to love and/or trust God. It's a simple issue of transference, to use a psych term. Our earthly father is our model of what and who a father is. If we had a great, loving relationship with our father, then it's easy for us to love and trust God. If we didn't have a great relationship with our father, then we find it difficult to have a good relationship with God. In our hearts and minds, a father is a father—one good, all good, or one bad, all bad. That's a very simplified statement, but it's true nonetheless. It's not my purpose to get into a psychological study in this book. I'm not qualified. There are many very good books on the subject. My personal favorite is *The Blessing* by John Trent and Gary Smalley. If you have been struggling with loving or trusting God, then I would ask you, "How was your relationship with your father?" Answer that question for yourself. Then you can decide if I'm right about this question of why you have your doubts about or issues with God.

The greatest source of our capacity to give and receive love is God. We are most able to love others when we are secure in our love from God. God created love. He is our love supply. When we are not sure of our love-source, then our supply of love and our capacity for love is compromised. If you still have doubts about God's unconditional love for you, talk to Him. Go to Him in prayer and share your concerns, your doubts and fears. He will answer you and reassure you of His complete commitment to you. Try it. You'll like it.

Love is multi-faceted. Within love are the best and most desirable qualities of our nature, the qualities that we observed in the life of Jesus Christ. Jesus' life was an exhibition of the character of love, because Jesus was love in human form. I want to discuss a few of the qualities of love so we can better understand the full scope and nature of Love.

Acceptance

Living a life of love begins with accepting one another for who we are, as we are. Since the beginning of man's existence, he has struggled to peacefully co-exist with his fellow man. Thousands of books have been written, and scores of laws have been enacted in an attempt to handle that issue. Man has even waged war in an attempt to achieve peace. Ponder that one for a moment, if you will … war to gain peace. Have you ever wondered why legions of men armed with all manner of destructive weapons have been called peace-keeping forces? We employ weapons and force to achieve peace? No wonder mankind has struggled through the centuries.

In order for us to learn acceptance, we must first unlearn a behavior that we've adopted. It's one to which we are unentitled and for which we are absolutely unqualified—judgment. Where judgment is, acceptance cannot be. Judgment is inappropriate and unfair. While we are recognizing our neighbor's faults, we are unable to see his qualities. The irony of judgment has been pointed out many times by psychologists, and accurately so, I might add. Usually, the behaviors that we tend to judge are the very ones that we would see in ourselves if we were to stand before the mirror of truth. Jesus pointed that out when He said:

> Hypocrite! First remove the plank from your own eye,
> and then you will see clearly to remove the
> speck from your brother's eye.
> Matthew 7:5

There is a lot of truth in the expression that when we are pointing out something about someone, three of our fingers are pointing back at ourselves. We are so very quick to point out the faults of others, while conveniently forgetting that we too are quite imperfect. We don't realize that when we engage ourselves in this distasteful pastime, we are setting ourselves up for exposure under the light of the Lord's judgment. Jesus warned us about that.

> Judge not, and you shall not be judged.
> Condemn not, and you shall not be condemned.
> Luke 6:37

Remember when your mother told you, "If you don't have something nice to say, don't say anything"? Heed her words; they are wise. Besides, when you criticize and judge others, you usually end up making yourself look small and petty. You can never make yourself bigger by trying to make someone else smaller. When you feel you are about to judge someone, instead, try to make a concerted effort to point out something positive about them. Praise them instead of criticizing them. You'll end up feeling better about both of you, and you'll add a little bit more love into the world at that moment. There was a popular song in the 1960s that said, "What the world needs now is love, sweet love." Those were words of truth, sweet truth.

Realizing that we were not able to accept one another, God sent His Son, the personification of love and acceptance, to save us from destroying each other. Jesus took a look around, gave it some thought, and in just thirteen words, He solved the entire problem.

> Therefore, whatever you want men to
> do to you, do also to them …
> Matthew 7:12

There it is, the truth. One sentence, one amazingly simple truth that settles once and for all how we can all accept each other and get along with one another. We know it as the Golden Rule. If you think about it logically, it makes perfect sense. What harm or bad thing can possibly come from following that idea? If I am trying to do the best for you, and you are trying to do the best for me, how then can we have any outcome other than that which is best for both of us?

When you "do unto others as you would have them do unto you," you create acceptance. You have, in effect, made them the same as you, by treating them as you would have yourself treated. You've acknowledged and accepted them as equals, as brothers, as fellow children of God, as someone worthy of compassion and love.

So why can't we do it? I believe it's because as in just about every other problem of mankind, we've gotten away from the truth—the truth that God created us to love Him, and to love one another. God showed us the way. First He gave us His rules of conduct. Then, He sent His Son to live among us as the perfect example of living a life of love. Jesus was and is the light of the world, love's true light. All we need to do is follow His light. Ah, there's the rub. We don't follow His example, because we think we have a better way. Well, this book is written for those of you who are willing to admit that maybe you don't have a better way. But with prayer and humble obedience, you can, as I did, find your way back to the truth, the truth of love. God showed us how we can experience lives full of joy, and the richness of love in the truest sense when He sent Jesus to live among us as the example of godly, eternal love.

Selflessness

Another great characteristic of love is that it is unselfish. Human "love" is often just the opposite. Man, by his nature, is selfish. He tends to look out for himself first. That, by definition, happens at the expense of others. It represents the antithesis of godly love, which puts the interests of others before itself. Consider these words from Jesus' teaching:

> Greater love has no man than this, than to
> lay down one's life for his friends
> John 15:13

That, of course, is taking love to the extreme. But the point to glean from that statement is that true love involves self-sacrifice, putting others' needs ahead of our own.

> Let nothing be done through selfish ambition or conceit,
> but in lowliness of mind let each esteem others better than himself.
> Philippians 2:3

Giving of ourselves usually results in us receiving even a greater blessing than that which we were trying to convey. I'm sure you can recall times when you deferred to another's desires, and how it made you feel. Perhaps you agreed to watch a movie with your wife instead of watching the game on a Sunday afternoon. Or perhaps you took your child to the park instead of playing golf with your buddies. When you chose to put that other person's desires ahead of your own, you felt a peaceful, contented happiness deep inside, didn't you? You were glad you did whatever it was, because you brought love and value to another person. As a result, you experienced an inner satisfaction that perhaps you couldn't explain. When you behave in a loving manner, you are in harmony with the energy of God. You are in tune with your true nature as a child of your loving Heavenly Father. There is a harmonious flow of love between you and the other person at that moment. You are living as you were intended to live because you allowed love to direct your heart and your actions. Our lives are at their best when we allow love and selflessness to be our guide and motivation.

> Let each of you look out not only for his own interests,
> but also for the interests of others.
> Philippians 2:4

As He did so many times, in so many situations, Jesus set the example for us. He backed up His words with His actions. It's easy to say we should consider others before ourselves, but Jesus actually lived it. Although Jesus was God incarnate, He was also fully human, with human fears and the capacity to feel human pain. On the eve of His crucifixion, which He knew was coming, He was praying in the Garden of Gethsemane. In a frightful moment of His humanity, when He was thinking of what He was about to face, He cried out to God, His Father, saying:

> "O My Father, if it is possible, let this cup pass from Me;
> nevertheless, not as I will, but as You will."
> Matthew 26:39

Jesus did not have to go through with His impending death. He certainly had the power to change the plan. His faith, His courage, His obedience, His love, and His respect for His Father gave Him the strength to fulfill His divinely ordained purpose. His

death was to be a sacrifice for our sins, *our* sins. He was without
sin. He endured that hideous death solely to save you and me. So,
my friend, when you are faced with an opportunity to sacrifice a
little for someone else, even if it's something as simple as going to
a movie you don't really want to see, please remember that any
act of self-sacrifice, no matter how large or small, is an expression
of love toward someone else. That person will feel more valuable,
and you will not go unrewarded one day. God may not remember
repented wrongs, but He does remember and reward good deeds.
Jesus said:

> do good, ... hoping for nothing in return;
> and your reward will be great
> Luke 6:35

This past summer, I was at a convenience store when I saw
an obviously poor, elderly couple struggling to get their beat-up
old car started. It was hot that day, I had nice clothes on, and I
didn't feel like getting sweaty or dirty. I started to drive away,
but that still, small voice inside me said, *Geoff, you know you've
got to help them.* I pulled my car in front of theirs, got out my
cables, and gave them a jump. Of course, they were very grateful.
But you know what? I couldn't stop smiling for hours after that.
That's the way it works. They received a blessing, but I received
a bigger one. As usual, Jesus had something to say about that as
well. It seems He had a lot to say about a lot of things, doesn't
it? Why not, He made it all, He knows what He's talking about.
Anyhow, He said:

> It's more blessed to give than to receive
> Acts 20:35

Yes, I know you've heard that a million times. But it's true, isn't it? So when the opportunity arises for you to step out of your way for a moment to help someone, do it. And when you have the choice of giving someone their preference over yours, give it. And when there's a need that you can fill, fill it.

> and then He will reward each according to his works.
> For the Son of Man will come in the glory
> of His Father with His angels,
> Matthew 16:27

Now you know that you will one day be rewarded for your good deeds. But don't do them in expectation of future rewards. Do them purely for the sake of being kind to a fellow human being.

Maybe this will convince you. Jesus takes your good deeds, or the lack thereof, personally. He was talking to a group of people about doing things to help others. Here's what He had to say.

> "Then the King will say to those on His right hand,
> 'Come, you blessed of My Father,
> inherit the kingdom prepared for you from
> the foundation of the world:
> for I was hungry and you gave Me food;
> I was thirsty and you gave Me drink; I was
> a stranger and you took Me in;
> I was naked and you clothed Me; I was sick and you visited Me;
> I was in prison and you came to Me.'
> "Then the righteous will answer Him, saying,
> 'Lord, when did we see You hungry and feed
> You, or thirsty and give You drink?
> When did we see You a stranger and take
> You in, or naked and clothe You?

Or when did we see You sick, or in prison, and come to You?'
And the King will answer and say to them, 'Assuredly, I say to you,
inasmuch as you did it to one of the least of these My brethren,
you did it to Me.'"
Matthew 25:34-40

What you do, and what you don't do, matters to God. In fact,
this passage goes on and talks about those who didn't do unto others.
It ends with this:

Assuredly, I say to you,
inasmuch as you did not do it to one of the least of these,
you did not do it to Me.
And these will go away into everlasting punishment,
but the righteous into eternal life.
Matthew 25:45-46

The rewards for giving are great; the consequences for withholding
are dire. Therefore, give, and live!

Forgiveness

Ouch! I may have hit a nerve. Forgiveness? *Geoff, you are going to
tell me I need to forgive everyone?* Yes! *But that's impossible; you don't
know what he did to me. You don't know the problems he caused me.*
You're right, I don't know. And you know what else? I don't care. I
don't mean that I don't care that you've been hurt. I mean I don't
care what the offense was. You must forgive—your own peace and
happiness depends on it.

Before I get too far into this discussion of forgiveness, which
is typically thought of as pertaining to forgiving others, I want
to talk about the most important aspect of forgiveness—forgiving
yourself.

One of the saddest, most debilitating situations in human life is when people can't or won't forgive themselves. Somehow, they have reached the point where because of their own guilt, shame, self-criticism, and self doubt, they believe they are so bad, or their deeds are so bad, that they cannot or should not be forgiven—either by God or themselves. I know about this. I've lived there. It is a miserable place to be. I had to learn the truth—God forgives everything and I am forgivable—before I could forgive myself. Dear reader, you too are forgivable. In this chapter I've talked about God's love for you. Believe me, He values you more than you can imagine. He sees you as lovable, and He wants to forgive you. He wants to restore you to right standing with Him. It is His desire to see you as clean, guiltless, and blameless. If you are struggling with this issue of self-forgiveness, then please read on and let God's truth be revealed to your heart and mind.

In Him we have redemption through His
blood, the forgiveness of sins,
according to the riches of His grace
Ephesians 1:7

When people believe themselves to be so bad as to be unforgivable, they condemn themselves to a life of unhappiness, unworthiness, and defeat. The real tragedy is that it is all unnecessary; they are operating under one of the cruelest lies. They carry the guilt and shame of a condemnation that doesn't exist. I say this because if those people had asked the Lord for forgiveness and they were sincere in the asking, then they were forgiven at that very moment. Their sins were wiped off the slate and their lives and their beings are clean again. They are free to begin anew in whatever aspect of their lives that was affected by their unnecessary guilt. But if they don't forgive themselves, then they remain imprisoned by their guilt, regrets, and self-recriminations—but it's only in their own mind that the prison walls exist. In truth, they are free, but for themselves. How tragic and sad. Those people cannot move on with the confidence and the peace of mind that forgiveness would have granted them. Actually, it was granted to them, only they don't realize it because of their own lack of self-forgiveness.

Another thought just occurred to me. What do you suppose the cross was for? Jesus died for your sins, remember? I'm not trying to be a wise guy here; I just want you to realize that the God of our universe, the Creator of you and me, has already paid the price specifically to free you from your guilt and sin. I'll remind you once again, dear reader, that God demonstrated very clearly how valuable you truly are to Him. God paid the price to buy forgiveness for you.

> He has delivered us from the power of darkness
> and conveyed us into the kingdom of the Son of His love,
> in whom we have redemption through His
> blood, the forgiveness of sins
> Colossians 1:13-14

It's done! Please accept it. It is God's amazing free gift to you simply because He loves you so much. God believes you are good enough to be forgiven; do you think He is wrong? If God has chosen to forgive you, then how can you believe that you shouldn't forgive yourself? If for no other reason than the pure logic behind it, please believe the truth that you are forgivable and therefore should forgive yourself. I may be repeating myself, but this is absolutely worth repeating as many times as it takes for you to learn the truth about God and you.

> And you, who once were alienated and enemies in your
> mind by wicked works, yet now He has reconciled in
> the body of His flesh through death, to present you holy,
> and blameless, and above reproach in His sight
> Colossians 1:21-22

There it is—the truth! Because of Jesus' love and sacrifice for you, you are now holy, blameless, and above reproach in His sight. You are forgiven once and for all.

Dear reader, if you are carrying guilt, shame, and regret about something that has been forgiven by the Lord and others, please let it go. You have been set free of your crime. God "remembers it no more." It's gone. You do not have to carry the burden. You are no longer restrained and restricted from freedom. You bear no guilt, owe no restitution. The issue is over, the case is closed. Please release yourself so that you can once again enjoy life, liberty, and the pursuit of happiness. God has granted you that freedom. Please realize His grace and mercy and accept that precious gift of forgiveness. You owe it to yourself and everyone with whom you interact. When you are bound by the lie of self-unforgiveness, your effectiveness as a human being is greatly compromised. You must be free yourself before you can ever help others find their freedom in truth.

Now that is settled, I'd like to talk about forgiving others. But first, this is a great opportunity for me give you a quick example of a lie versus the truth and how it can have a dramatic effect on your life. Some people resist forgiveness because they think it shows weakness. That's the lie. They believe that a strong person doesn't just take it, but rather, he seeks revenge to exact retribution on his attacker. Jesus feels differently about that. Look at His words on the subject.

> You have heard that it was said, 'An eye for
> an eye and a tooth for a tooth.
> But I tell you not to resist an evil person.
> But whoever slaps you on your right cheek,
> turn the other to him also.
> Matthew 5:38-39

The truth is that restraint and forgiveness demonstrate real strength of mind and character. Anyone can react and lash out. The genuinely strong man controls his mind and his actions.

I'd like to make a point here. If you are reading these verses and thinking, *Well that's nice, but I'm going to handle things my way,* you are thinking unwisely. Let me give you a very specific example. I know a young man who was wronged by another man. Later, this young man went after his abuser to seek revenge in the form of a physical beating. During the course of the event, the young man injured his shoulder to the extent that it caused him to require surgery, and the damage was not able to be completely repaired. He now has a permanent injury to his shoulder. There is a price to pay if you ignore God's teaching.

Vengeance is a poor choice—nobody wins. You simply end up with two offenders and two victims. And the truth is, you don't have to seek revenge. You have someone to handle that for you.

for it is written, "Vengeance is mine, I will repay," says the Lord
Romans 12:19

Remember, we are all imperfect beings. We all live in glass houses, and we all are in need of forgiveness. It is best if we just drop the rocks, and pray that our brothers will do the same. Further, God actually rewards you when go so far as to be kind to those who hurt you.

If your enemy is hungry, give him bread to eat;
And if he is thirsty, give him water to drink;
For so you will heap coals of fire on his head,
And the Lord will reward you
Proverbs 25:21-22

Why would God reward us? Because He wants to reinforce to us how important love and forgiveness are to the well being of us. Where ill will and unforgiveness exist, love and peace cannot. Also, and more importantly, God knows that none of us are innocent, and as such, are therefore unqualified to judge or condemn anyone. Do you remember the story of the woman caught in adultery? A group of very arrogant, self-righteous religious leaders brought a woman to Jesus in the hope that He would condemn her. Instead, Jesus responded out of love and understanding—the way we should respond whenever possible.

the Pharisees brought to Him a woman caught in adultery …
they said to Him, "Teacher, this woman was caught in adultery, …
the law commanded us that such should
be stoned. But what do You say?"
… He raised Himself up and said to them,
"He who is without sin among you, let
him throw a stone at her first."
John 8:3-7

No stones were thrown that day.

One by one those men sheepishly walked away. They had been convicted within themselves by their own guilt and lack of compassion and forgiveness. But, that wasn't the end of the episode. What follows is a touching example of what Jesus is all about – love and forgiveness. After the men left, He turned to the woman and said:

"Woman, where are those accusers of yours?
Has no one condemned you?"
She said, "No one, Lord."
And Jesus said to her, "Neither do I condemn
you; go and sin no more."
John 8:10-11

For me, the true beauty of this story is not in what was said, but what was not said. It is a classic example of the heart of Jesus. The situation was a ready made opportunity for teaching about sin. But Jesus never condemned the woman or lectured her on her wrong doings. He knew quite well that she understood her sin and was already humiliated. Rather than add to her woes, Jesus chose to express tender forgiveness and love to her. He knows that we are not perfect, and reminding us of our short comings will not heal our sin or help us grow. It would simply add to our guilt. Only love and understanding can heal us.

Are you beginning to see who Jesus is; are you appreciating His nature? I wonder how you or I would have handled that situation. Would we have been so compassionate and understanding? The more I study Jesus, the more I realize He is the ultimate role model. I want to become more like Him – as much as is possible.

Jesus gave us many excellent teachings on forgiveness, by His words and His example. In what I think was probably His greatest example of strength and forgiveness, Jesus, as He was hanging on the cross, said these words:

> Father, forgive them, for they know not what they do.
> Luke 23:34 (NIV)

Can you really imagine that? He was speaking of men who had tortured Him, and then had driven spikes through His wrists and ankles to crucify Him! In a moment of unspeakable misery, Jesus, because of His love, because He *is* Love, was pleading for the lives of the very people who were trying to kill Him. That, my friends, is love and forgiveness at its highest.

Forgiveness should be given freely and unconditionally. Would you feel forgiven if someone said, "I forgive you" and then went on to remind you of what you did and how much you hurt them? No, you'd feel guilty all over again. Well, neither will someone who has wronged you feel forgiven if you don't let the offense go. Forgive and move on; that's how God handles it.

> For I will forgive their iniquity, and their
> sin I will remember no more
> Jeremiah 31:34

Speaking for myself, I am truly grateful that when God forgives, He "remembers no more." Have you done some things that you would prefer were forgotten? Of course you have, so pass that same blessing on to others. Remember the words from God's description of love—"it keeps no record of wrong doings."

Here are a few questions for you to consider regarding forgiveness.

Do I have to forgive everything?

David described God as one:

> "who forgives **all** your iniquities"
> Psalm 103

Paul, in his letter to the Colossians wrote:

> "And you, being dead in your trespasses,
> ... He has made alive together
> with Him, having forgiven you **all** trespasses"
> Colossians 2:13

I hope you appreciate the fact that God forgives everything. What if He didn't? Which of your sins would you want Him to remember? It is logical that He would remember the ones that made the biggest impression—the worst ones. Therefore, let's all be thankful that His forgiveness is complete. Please make sure your forgiveness is complete as well.

How many times must I forgive someone? Jesus said we should forgive:

up to seventy times seven

Matthew 18:22

I suspect He didn't mean 490 times. I believe He meant as many times as it takes.

Is there any consequence for me if I don't forgive? Here's what Jesus said about that:

but if you do not forgive men their trespasses,
neither will your Father forgive your trespasses.
Matthew 6:15

That is a very direct—no room for discussion—statement. Do you want to face God's punishment for your sins?

Additionally, there is a more immediate consequence for unforgiveness. When you don't forgive an offense, you inadvertently hold onto all the anger, hurt, bitterness, and pain that came with it. Guess who that affects. Not the other person; they've probably forgotten about the whole thing. Those negative thoughts and emotions will hurt *you*. They are malignancies that will eat you from the inside out. For your own sake, let them go.

Forgiveness, like all of God's ideas, creates a win-win situation. It is absolutely necessary in any interpersonal relationship. Forgiveness shows compassion and understanding for the person who offended you. In other words, it shows love. In fact, forgiveness is an act of love. The truth is, most of the time when people have offended you, they are sorry for what they've done, and you can free them from their guilt and shame by offering your forgiveness. In cases where the other person doesn't care that he or she hurt you, or his or her offense was intentional, then your forgiveness becomes a gift to yourself. When you forgive, you release yourself from the pain and hurt of the offense. Forgiveness, like truth, will set you free.

Any relationship will begin to dissolve after the very first offense if there is no forgiveness. Without forgiveness, anger and resentment will grow quickly with each additional offense until the relationship is intolerable. If you want to live a life of love and peace and happiness, learn to forgive every time, all the time.

As you grow in God's love, you will find that forgiveness comes more easily to you. And each time you forgive someone, you gain a little more love and peace in your own life.

We've looked at a few of the qualities of love. Love is such an all-encompassing concept that if I were to attempt to comprehensively explore it, this volume would become absurdly unwieldy, and I want to address other topics, so I'll end this chapter here.

Dear reader, please, whenever possible, adopt a loving attitude to every person you encounter, and in every situation, take a loving approach. When you do, your life will be just a little sweeter, a little kinder, a little happier, and a lot more loving. In other words, it'll just be better for everyone concerned.

Here are some very wise, love-filled words from the apostle Paul.

But above all these things put on love, ...
And let the peace of God rule in your hearts ...
Colossians 3:14-15

And now abide faith, hope, love, these three;
but the greatest of these is love
1 Corinthians 13:13

✝

FAITH

Of Things Unseen

"Now faith is the substance of things hoped for,
the evidence of things not seen"
Hebrews 11:1

That is one of my favorite verses in the Bible. I love it for its literary elegance and for its message. Faith is the capacity to believe in that which you cannot see, hear, taste, or feel. Logic and reason cannot explain it, but your heart tells you it's so. That's interesting. Logic and reason are products of the mind. Faith is an affair of the heart. When you came into being, God planted the seed of faith in your heart. He did that to give you a little head start.

But God gives it a body as He pleases,
and to each seed it's own body.
1 Corinthians 15:38

The "seed" is a little bit of the essence of God that was placed in you at conception—when you began your life as a little tiny embryonic human. From there, it's up to you to feed and water your little seed so it can blossom into the faith that will carry you through your life.

Whether you realize it or not, faith is the cornerstone of your life. In many ways, it is what allows you to move throughout your day. When you are driving, you are exercising unexpressed faith that the other drivers will perform correctly. When you walk up a flight of stairs, you are acting in faith that they won't collapse. When you eat at a restaurant, you've confessed your faith that the food is safe. Almost everything you do is done in faith of some sort. You certainly are a very trusting soul, aren't you? But I wonder, have you placed your faith and trust in the only Being in existence that is truly worthy of your faith and trust? Of all the things in which you can put your faith, only God and Jesus are always faithful, always trustworthy. Anything else, everyone else, can fail you. God will not fail you—ever.

Therefore know that the Lord your God,
He is God, the faithful God who keeps covenant and mercy ...
with those who love Him and keep His commandments
Deuteronomy 7:9

God is faithful,
by whom you were called into the fellowship of His Son,
Jesus Christ our Lord.
1 Corinthians 1:9

... the Lord is faithful, who will establish you and
guard you from the evil one."
2 Thessalonians 3:3

Therefore I have hope.
Through the Lords' mercies we are not consumed,
Because His compassions fail not.
They are new every morning;
Great is Your faithfulness.
Lamentations 3:21-23

Do you remember the Psalm I used at the start of this book?

Yea, though I walk through the valley of the shadow of death,
I will fear no evil, for you are with me
Psalm 23

David, in an eloquent statement, was expressing his faith in God. If you want to enjoy your birthright as a child of God, you must accept God as faithful and trustworthy. He is your refuge of last resort. When all else in life fails you, God will not. You can depend on Him every time, all the time. Without Him, you have nothing. With Him, you have everything. When you put your trust in God, you can move about in confidence, knowing that the most powerful Being in the universe loves you and is looking out for you.

If you are reading this book because you are looking to improve the quality of your life, you can begin to do so quickly by adopting one simple attitude—the attitude of *faith* in God.

For we walk by faith, not by sight.
2 Corinthians 5:7

When you focus your sight on your obstacles, you lose power because the energy of your mind is being expended on thinking about how or why something may go wrong. Conversely, when your mind is filled with faith, you tap into the unlimited power of God—

the power to overcome your obstacles. Train yourself to always walk by faith, and those mountainous obstacles will amazingly shrink to manageable molehills.

Doubt, worry, fear, and hopelessness are all symptoms of a lack of faith in God. Paradoxically, it takes more faith to put your trust in something other than God in any situation or circumstance. Anything else could be, or go, wrong. Only God cannot be wrong and cannot fail.

It does not make much sense not to have faith in God, but that's the way most people live. However, you don't have to be like most people. You can, as I've already said, become free of the stress of life's troubles by living in the confident knowledge of the truth that you can trust God, your Creator. Note: I said free of the stress of troubles. You will still have your troubles, but you can have less stress and more confidence when you are going through them.

Jesus looked at them and said to them,
With men this is impossible, but with God all things are possible.
Matthew 19:26

Remember that God's word is alive and relevant to you today. If Jesus said all things are possible with God, then all things are possible with God! His words of truth have not changed between the times He spoke them and now when you are reading them. When you feel that things are looking bad for you, when problems seem too big or too hard to solve, stop and ask God for help. Train yourself in that idea. As soon as you start feeling that nervous, worried feeling that we all know too well, just *stop*. Remember who is in charge, and talk to Him about your situation. I'll bet you've heard the expression, "There's nothing new under the sun." That is true. Somewhere in time, someone has been through whatever you're going through.

Your situation is certainly not new to God, and it didn't catch Him by surprise. He knew it was going to happen before it did. And He knows how to handle it, no matter what the circumstance. The only thing standing between you and the solution is you. Get out of the way and let God lead you in the right direction. He knows the way, and He'll lead you if you ask Him. That is what faith is about. That is the truth!

In another of His concise, power-filled statements, Jesus told us that the degree of our faith determines the reward of our faith.

> According to your faith let it be to you
> Matthew 9:29

The more faith you choose to have, the better you can make your life. Does faith give you power? Not directly. What your faith does is make more of God's power accessible to you because of your faith. Even Jesus, as a man, declared His need for the power He derived from His Father.

> I can of Myself do nothing,
> because I do not seek My own will
> but the will of the Father who sent Me.
> John 5:30

It is critical that you understand the truth that's central to that statement. For you to receive any power from your faith or your prayers, they must be consistent with God's will. If your neighbor angers you and you pray for harm to befall him, don't expect it to happen. Conversely, if you want God's guidance on finding a job or making an important decision, ask with prayerful expectation, and you'll receive an answer.

> For assuredly, I say to you, whoever says to this mountain,
> 'Be removed and be cast into the sea,'
> and does not doubt in his heart,
> but believes that those things he says will be done,
> he will have whatever he says.
> Mark 11:23

Remember, the degree or capacity of your faith determines the results of your faith. If you have absolute faith without any shadow of a doubt, nothing will be impossible to you (as long as it aligns with God's will).

I realize that doubt-free faith is easier spoken about than achieved, but if we can achieve it, there will be no limit to what we can do. We know this is true because of what Jesus did. His faith was without doubt, and nothing was impossible to Him. He performed acts that we refer to as miraculous. They were certainly beyond anything ever witnessed up until that time. What gave Him that power? His faith!

Consider these verses about people who had complete faith in Jesus. They are great examples of, "According to your faith, let it be to you." In these examples, we find three people with three different problems—bleeding, blindness, and sin—but they all had one thing in common—faith. And in each case Jesus told them that it was because of their faith that He helped them.

> … Jesus answered and said to him,
> "What do you want Me to do for you?"
> The blind man said to Him, "Rabbi, that I may receive my sight."
> Then Jesus said to him, "Go your way;
> your faith has made you well."
> And immediately he received his sight …
> Mark 10:51-52

A woman who had a flow of blood for
twelve years came from behind
and touched the hem of His garment. For she said to herself,
"If only I may touch His garment, I shall be made well."
But Jesus turned around, and when He saw her He said,
"Be of good cheer, daughter; your faith has made you well."
And the woman was made well from that hour.
Matthew 9:20-22

Do you see this woman? ...
I say to you, her sins, which are many, are forgiven ...
Then He said to her, "Your sins are forgiven."
... Your faith has saved you. Go in peace"
Luke 7:44-50

God means business. Believe in Him, have faith in Him, and
He'll do anything for you, even die for you. In fact, He did. But deny
Him, and He'll let you go on by yourself. Good luck with that!

But without faith it is impossible to please Him,
for he who comes to God must believe that He is,
and that He is a rewarder of those who diligently seek Him.
Hebrews 11:6

If you're wondering how your faith is doing, take a quick inventory
of your thoughts. If you're usually confident and optimistic, your
faith is probably in pretty good shape. If you find that you worry
a lot and have more than occasional doubts and fears, your faith is
probably lacking. But that condition can be remedied. Prayerfully,
seek to understand the word of God, let His truth permeate your
mind, and your faith will grow.

Along with your faith, God wants your faithfulness. When He gives you power in your life, He wants to know that He can trust you to use it for His will.

He raised up for them David as king,
to whom also He gave testimony and said, 'I have found David …
a man after My own heart, who will do all My will.'
Acts 13:22

God chose David to be king over His people, because He knew He could trust David. He knew David as a man "who will do all My will." David, interestingly, is the only biblical character who was described as "a man after God's own heart."

When you prove yourself faithful, God will increase His blessings to you, because you become trustworthy in His eyes.

'Well done, good and faithful servant;
you were faithful over a few things,
I will make you ruler over many things.
Enter into the joy of your Lord.'
Matthew 25:21

If you want to experience God's blessings, align yourself with His will, surrender to His guidance, and live by faith in Him.

The just shall live by faith."
Romans 1:17

Faith sustains you, and propels you onward through the trials of this life. The reward of a faithful life is this:

In this you greatly rejoice, … that the genuineness of your faith,
being much more precious than gold, …
may be found to praise, honor, and glory
at the revelation of Jesus Christ,
whom having not seen, you love.
Though now you do not see Him, yet believing,
you rejoice with joy inexpressible and full of glory,
receiving the end of your faith - the salvation of your souls.
1 Peter: 6-9

There you have it. Faith in God is essential to your existence, both now and later. It allows you to live confidently and hopefully in this life, and it's a key part of your ticket to the next one.

Finally, when you do choose to live by faith, you gain the second of the three principles Faith, Hope and Love as discussed by Paul – Hope. With faith, you have confidence that no matter how desperate a situation may seem, you can always have hope. With hope, you have the realization that a positive outcome is possible. And with the optimism that hope brings, you tend to be calmer during adversity and more able to think clearly and make better decisions. It all begins with Faith.

✝

PRAYER

Talking to God

God has given us many gifts. Among them, one in particular stands out for me—prayer. God has allowed us to talk to Him. Think about that. The all-powerful Creator of the universe is willing to let us speak to Him and He will patiently and lovingly listen to us. As a result, we have access to the greatest mind in existence. We can get the answer to any question, the solution to any problem, advice in any situation, and comfort in any trial. God is truly our loving heavenly Father. No matter where or when, if we need Him, He is there for us. So many people think of God, if they think of Him at all, as this big, scary, unreachable deity that we dare not disturb. Those people are left, or so they believe, to fend for themselves in this life. Nothing could be further from the truth. God is right here, right now when we need Him. In fact, He has encouraged us to call on Him at any time.

... pray without ceasing, ... for this is the will of God ...
1 Thessalonians 5:16-17

...in everything by prayer ... let your requests be made known to God
Philippians 4:6

... men always ought to pray and not lose heart ...
Luke 18:1

I desire therefore that the men pray everywhere
I Timothy 2:8

Is anyone among you suffering? Let him pray.
James 5:13

Prayer is essential for us to live successfully. Life is too confusing, too unpredictable, too unrelenting, too random, too impersonal, too impartial, and too dangerous for us to go it alone. We unquestionably need the wisdom and advice of someone wiser and more experienced than ourselves.

I can tell you from personal experience that prayer does in fact work. You can ask God for help and receive an answer. Many times I've asked God for help with something, or for advice or assistance with an important decision, and He's answered my prayer and helped me. One time in particular comes to mind. I'll share it, because since it came to mind, God must want me to share it for the benefit of someone reading this right now. I realize that this is an example of a minor issue, but the effect made such an impression on me that I remember it to this day. I was in college, and on this particular day, I was incredibly stressed about something. I don't remember what just now, but I remember the episode. It was the kind of feeling where I was nauseous, fearful, and overwhelmed. I remember going out on the back terrace and sitting on a lawn chair and just asking God to please help me calm down so I could think clearly and try to figure out what was wrong. I prayed as hard as I can ever remember praying. I dozed off briefly, and when I awoke I was suddenly aware of an incredible feeling of peace and confidence. There can be no doubt that God had touched me. I remember thinking, *Wow, this is amazing.* I had gone from a near-panic state to being absolutely calm in a matter of a minute or two. At that moment, I couldn't have worried if I tried. God had changed my state of being from total unrest to complete peace. I share this with you so you can believe that God does answer prayer and that you can actually feel His presence when you ask Him in faith.

The effective, fervent prayer of a righteous man avails much.
James 5:16

Jesus told us that there is power in praying together. Whenever possible, I encourage you to get with someone and ask him or her to pray with you.

Again I say to you that if two of you agree on earth
concerning anything that they ask,
it will be done for them by My Father in heaven.
For where two or three are gathered together in My name,
I am there in the midst of them.
Matthew 18:19-20

When you pray, your prayer does not have to be in some formal, orderly, structured manner of speech. You don't have to sound like a preacher when you talk to God. I've heard people try to pray in some pious style that obviously isn't how they would talk to you or me. They think that they need to pray that way in order for God to hear them. God is not impressed by your style; He is impressed by your sincerity. Just speak to Him from your heart. He knows you and He understands you. He doesn't want to hear some rote prayer that you memorized and rehearsed. Jesus commented on that very thing.

> And when you pray, do not use vain repetitions as the heathen do.
> For they think that they will be heard for their many words.
> Therefore do not be like them.
> For your Father knows the things you have
> need of before you ask Him.
> Matthew 6:7-8

Jesus gave us an example of prayer when He was teaching His disciples to pray. We know it as the Lord's Prayer. I believe it's actually a format, an outline for prayer. First, I'll present the prayer, and then I'll discuss the pattern for prayer that He was teaching. Jesus said: "In this manner, therefore, pray":

> Our Father in heaven,
> Hallowed be Your name.
> Your kingdom come.
> Your will be done
> On earth as it is in heaven.
> Give us this day our daily bread.
> And forgive us our debts,
> As we forgive our debtors.
> And do not lead us into temptation,
> But deliver us from the evil one.
> For Yours is the kingdom
> and the power and the glory forever. Amen
> Matthew 6:9-13

As you will see, each line concerns a new topic, on which you can expand as you talk to God and make your needs known to Him. In this "outline," Jesus told us that our prayers should begin with an acknowledgment of God as our loving Heavenly Father who is worthy of our praise.

"Our Father, who art in Heaven, Hallowed be Your Name"

Too many times we jump right in and begin our prayers with our laundry list of requests. We treat God as if He were a giant genie of whom we can simply ask for anything without regard for the genie himself. God is God. We must never take Him for granted. Yes, we are free to approach Him, but we must do so with respect and appreciation of the fact that He is our God, and we are fortunate indeed that He has granted us the privilege of coming to Him with our needs and requests.

Jesus continues with an understanding that whatever we are going to ask must be consistent with God's way and His will.

"Your kingdom come. Your will be done
on earth, as it is in heaven. "

God is the ultimate moral compass. He knows what is right and what is best for us and for His eternal plan. He wants to bless us with many blessings, but He will not be untrue to Himself. This isn't a Scripture verse, but it just came to me, so I'm sharing it with you—you ask in vain, if you ask not in the Father's will.

Once we have made it clear to God that we understand the program, we can then make our requests—first, for our basic necessities, and then for whatever else it is that we think we want or need.

"Give us this day our daily bread."

There is no limit to what God can do for you, if you will just ask. Often, His response to your prayer will come as a complete surprise to you. It may be entirely different from what you had in mind. That is usually followed by you thinking, *God, what is this? This is not want I wanted.* Maybe not, but you can bet it's better than what you wanted. As I've said earlier, God frequently has to intervene to save us from ourselves. You know the old saying "the best laid plans of mice and men"? Many times, when I thought I had a plan and asked God to bless it, He came back with a drastic revision or a complete cancellation of my plan. Have you had that experience? If so, it's your confirmation that God really is looking out for you. You may not understand His way, or even agree with it at first. That's okay. Just trust that He does care for you, and believe that He will help you to have what you truly need and desire—as He sees fit. He knows you far better than you know yourself. Don't forget, He made you. He knows what's inside the cover.

Next, and this is very important, we must clear up any issues we may have with God or our brothers, and they against us.

"And forgive us our debts, as we forgive our debtors."

How can we enter into a love conversation with God when we are full of malice toward our brother? I've already discussed the importance of forgiveness with you, so we should be in agreement on that point. Jesus said this:

Whenever you stand praying, if you have anything against anyone,
forgive him, that your Father in heaven may
also forgive you your trespasses
Mark 11:25

The next phrase of the prayer handles an issue that is central to our lives—Sin. Sin is the most fatal of all diseases. But there is also a sure cure for it—prayer.

"And do not lead us into temptation, but
deliver us from the evil one."

We have inherited from our ancestors the nature of sin. We don't necessarily try to sin; it just comes naturally to us. It's effortless for us to sin. The effort comes when we try to live rightly in the will of God. We cannot do it by ourselves. It's impossible. Jesus came to give us life, and He knows that sin can take our lives. That is precisely why He included this idea in His format for our prayers. He knows that only through Him can we be victorious over the deadly allure of sin.

Finally, we end by again praising our Almighty God, the Supreme Being who shall rule over us in His glorious power for all eternity:

> "For Yours is the kingdom and the power
> and the glory forever. Amen."

You can see that each phrase of the prayer is a topic for you to expand on as you pray. It's up to you to fill in whatever details are appropriate for you and your circumstances each day.

I learned this prayer, as many of us did, when I was a child. To me then, it was just something to be memorized. Today, it is something I hold in awe. The brilliance of Jesus continues to amaze me, even though by now, I should expect it, since He is God. Time after time, He is able in a few words to sum up and communicate volumes of information and wisdom. In the few phrases of that prayer, Jesus handled every issue about which we would ever need to approach God for help. Anything you might ever need to ask Him will fit within one of those topics. The next time you go to pray, start with His outline, say the words of each line, and then add your own words as they fit. See if you don't notice a feeling of completeness in your prayer, a feeling that you've actually communicated with God. Jesus never wasted time or words. If He took the time to teach us those words, then you can rest assured that they are worthwhile, and they will help you.

Please, do not fail to pray. In every situation or circumstance, call on Him. Let Him help you, comfort you, guide you, and bless you. He will hear your prayers, and He will answer them. Trust Him on that.

> For the eyes of the Lord are on the righteous,
> And His ears are open to their prayers
> 1 Peter 3:12

> And whatever things you ask in prayer,
> believing, you will receive.
> Matthew 21:22

†

WISDOM

Not what or how much you know

Wisdom is not what you know or how much you know. There are a lot of very well-educated individuals who lack wisdom. Knowledge is wonderful, but if it's not accompanied by wisdom, it's not worth a whole lot. On the other hand, you can lack knowledge and education and yet be very wise.

Let's see what dictionary.com says:

Knowledge: acquaintance with facts, truths, or principles, as from study or investigation.

Wisdom: the quality or state of being wise; knowledge of what is true or right coupled with just judgment as to action.

Those are pretty good definitions. Do you see the distinction between the two? Knowledge is knowing things; wisdom is knowing how to apply your knowledge in the way that is best for all concerned.

The man who is generally considered to be one of the wisest men who ever lived is Solomon, a biblical writer. He wrote three books in the Bible—Proverbs, Ecclesiastes, and Song of Solomon. I will be using several of his verses in this chapter.

You may already be familiar with some of Solomon's words without realizing it. They were used in a popular song from the 1960s written by Pete Seeger and recorded by the Byrds—"Turn, Turn, Turn—to Everything There Is a Season" (from Ecclesiastes). I thought you might like that bit of trivia.

Wisdom is an innate sense of truth, of right and wrong, of how things should be, of things that matter and things that don't. Wisdom is the ability to sort out the meaningful from the meaningless. Wisdom allows you to make sense of and understand life. Wisdom is when you know that you know that you know—you know? Sorry, I couldn't resist that one. Anyhow, wisdom is truly something to be desired.

God wants us to have wisdom, He knows how much more meaningful our lives can be both to ourselves and to others when we have wisdom. As I was researching for this chapter, I came across something that I hadn't seen before. It showed me just how much God values wisdom and how much He appreciates it when we are wise enough to ask Him to grant us wisdom. Solomon had been praying, and asking God for wisdom. Here is God's reply.

> Now give me wisdom and knowledge ...
> Then God said to Solomon:
> "Because this was in your heart, and you have
> not asked riches or wealth or honor ...
> nor have you asked long life - but have
> asked wisdom and knowledge
> for yourself, that you may judge My people
> over whom I have made you king,

wisdom and knowledge are granted to
you; and I will give you riches
and wealth and honor,
such as none of the kings have had who were before you,
nor shall any after you have the like."
2 Chronicles 1:10-12

The next verse I'm going to share is one of my favorites. I try to live by it. For example, each morning when I wake up, I read some Scripture and pray before I do anything else. I was just trying to follow the advice of the verse. I didn't realize how potent the verse from Matthew was until I came across the one about Solomon and God. Read this verse.

But seek first the kingdom of God and His righteousness,
and all these things shall be added to you.
Matthew 6:33

Solomon was asking only for wisdom, and God blessed Him beyond his wildest imagination. That should be a lesson to all of us. Out of our selfish desires, we tend to ask for worldly things, rather than godly things. God knows what we need as opposed to what we think we want. Perhaps, if we were to ask Him for what He thinks is important, two good things might happen. 1. He would supply our needs with the things He knows are truly important that will make real differences in our lives, and 2. He will surprise us by giving us the desires of our hearts. I think it comes down to a matter of trust. Do you trust God enough to ask Him to give you what He knows is best for you?

Try starting by asking Him for wisdom. I can think of a couple good reasons. The first is it's clear He wants you to be wise. Second, when you gain wisdom, you may find yourself asking for very different things. Why? When you are asking from the perspective of wisdom, you will be asking for things that truly will be meaningful and beneficial to you—as opposed to the things that you've thought you wanted, and later learned were not such a good idea. One thing is for sure, you cannot get hurt by asking God for wisdom. You'll just start seeing things as they really are, and you'll be able to discern truth from untruth. That in itself is worth the effort. Think of all the future problems and mistakes you can avoid if you become in tune with the wisdom of God.

As I've sought wisdom and the will of God, my thoughts and my desires have changed greatly. Many of the things that I once thought were important now seem less important, and in some cases, even silly. It's not unlike when we change from being children into adults. The things that we think about and desire change right along with us. So as we gain wisdom, our thoughts and desires change as well. I don't claim to be especially wise, but I can say that I have a greater understanding of life and the world than I had before I started seeking wisdom, and the kind of knowledge that God wants me to have.

Look at these words from the first chapter of Solomon's proverbs:

> To know wisdom and instruction,
> To perceive the words of understanding,
> To receive the instruction of wisdom,
> Justice, judgment, and equity;
> To give prudence to the simple,
> To the young man knowledge and discretion
> A wise man will hear and increase learning,
> And a man of understanding will attain wise counsel,
> The fear of the Lord is the beginning of knowledge,
> But fools despise wisdom and instruction.
> Proverbs 1:2-7

I don't want to be numbered among the fools, so I will continue to ask the Lord to lead me into wisdom. Here are some words from the second chapter of Proverbs:

> So that you incline your ear to wisdom,
> And apply your heart to understanding;
> Yes, if you cry out for discernment,
> And lift up your voice for understanding,
> If you seek her as silver,
> And search for her as for hidden treasures;
> And find the knowledge of God.
> For the Lord gives wisdom;
> From His mouth come knowledge and understanding;
> He stores up sound wisdom for the upright;
> Proverbs 2:1-7

All of us at various times in our lives will need help and advice on something. There are many apparently wise people to whom you can go for counsel. But I want to caution you: even the best of us are incapable of being completely detached, impartial, and objective.

When you take advice from someone, be aware that no matter how well intentioned that person may be, whatever he or she says to you must come through the filter of his or her mind, with all its prejudices, experiences, biases, attitudes, and beliefs. Listen to the words of your confidante, but then go to the Lord, and ask Him what He thinks. Check what your human friend said against the word of God. If the two don't align, if they aren't in agreement, please be careful. When in doubt, listen to your own inner voice, that still, small voice that speaks inside you. If you've been praying and asking God, then you can be pretty confident that the still, small voice that seems to be your own innate wisdom is actually the voice of God talking to you. The more you talk to God and begin to trust Him, the more you'll also begin to trust yourself. You'll trust your own wisdom, because you'll have the assurance that it's coming from God.

Remember, we're all born with blank slates in our minds. As we live and go through life, we accumulate knowledge and hopefully wisdom as well. The people who have wisdom got it because they humbled themselves and were willing to learn from God. They opened their minds to Him, and He gave them wisdom. He will do the same for you if you just ask Him. Believe me, you want wisdom more than you want gold or silver, or any other material accumulations. Without wisdom, any "gold" that you own can be dangerous. You'll just have more ability to get yourself and possibly others into trouble. On the other hand, when you have wisdom, you'll be able to get so much more out of your resources. God is the greatest investment counselor you'll ever find. Please realize that I'm not talking only about conventional investments here. I'm talking about anything that you might possess, be it a skill, a talent, or knowledge. Wouldn't you like to have God's influence working with you when you are in a position to lead, influence, or assist others in some way?

> Happy is the man who finds wisdom,
> And the man who gains understanding;
> For her proceeds are better than the profits of silver,
> And her gain than fine gold.
> Proverbs 3:13-14

Wisdom allows you to make proper, intelligent choices in your life. I'm sure you've heard the expression, "Fools rush in." I can assure you I've rushed in far too many times. It wasn't until I finally thought to ask God for some of His wisdom that I learned to look (and pray) before I leaped.

Every day, we are all faced with many choices and decisions. Some are minor, simple, and obvious. Some are much more complex and carry with them great consequences, positive or negative, depending which path we choose. It's the latter group of which I speak when I say that is when we should seek God's wisdom on the matter. The great thing about God, unlike even our most trusted human friend(s), is He is never wrong, and He will never lead us into something that can be harmful to us. When we seek human counsel, we are taking a chance. Even our most trusted confidante who has the best of intentions can simply be mistaken and could influence us into disastrous circumstances.

Dear reader, when you encounter a situation about which you have even a slight doubt or question, please take a moment and ask God what He thinks about it. You may not sense an audible response, but God will speak to your heart and mind. Then when you make your choice or decision, you'll know if it's right or wrong, by the feeling in your gut. And my friends, if it doesn't feel right, please think twice about it. Oh how I wish I had trusted my gut feeling on so many things in the past. Now, when I have "that feeling," I listen to it every time. To ignore to the coaxing of God is to court disaster. When in doubt, go with your gut.

> When wisdom enters your heart,
> And knowledge is pleasant to your soul,
> Discretion will preserve you;
> Understanding will keep you,
> To deliver you from the way of evil,
> Proverbs 2:10-12

I'll end this chapter with these rather enthusiastic words from Solomon about his favorite mistress—Wisdom

Get wisdom! Get understanding!
Do not forget, nor turn away from the words of my mouth.
Do not forsake her, and she will preserve you;
Love her, and she will keep you.
Wisdom is the principal thing;
Therefore get wisdom.
And in all your getting, get understanding.
Exalt her, and she will promote you;
She will bring you honor, when you embrace her.
Proverbs 4:5-8

†

HOPE

Fear not

Some of the worst times of my life were when I felt hopeless in a situation. Fear overtook my mind. Reason and logic were inaccessible to me. My mind was useless as a source of solution. I couldn't think. I could only sit, almost frozen, in a state of mental impotence. It was scary and very distressing. Have you ever felt that way? Hopelessness is about the worst state of mind in which one can find oneself. Without hope, we lose the strength to continue, and we cannot keep going. When hope is lost, our future is lost. We believe that any effort expended would be wasted, so why even try? Hopelessness is deadly to the mind and spirit. It is because of the danger of hopelessness that God gives us Hope. He knows we need it to have a reason to persist. Hope is the light at the end of the tunnel. It's the beacon that draws us forward, no matter how perilous things may seem. Hope gives us renewed strength when strength has been exhausted. Hope keeps our thoughts going when we are at the end of mental endurance. Hope is the last resort of the desperate. Hope is sometimes all we have left.

What Is Hope?

Hope is the truth of God placed in our hearts to sustain us when otherwise, all would seem lost. Hope is the thought that somehow that which we desire can come about. It's a belief that when all is said and done, our wants and needs will be fulfilled. God created Hope for us because without it, we are in great jeopardy. The ultimate consequence of complete loss of hope is suicide. When a person has lost all expectation of recovery from a situation, when there appears to be absolutely no way out of a circumstance, when every conceivable option is negative, then life becomes unendurable and completely undesirable. I grieve when I hear of someone who has lost hope and has performed the final act of hopelessness. If only they would have known the truth, the truth that literally could have saved their life.

Hopelessness may well be the ultimate lie, the deadliest untruth. Here is the Truth:

With God, nothing is hopeless

How do I know that is true? I know it because the Author of truth told us:

Jesus looked at them and said to them,

With men this is impossible, but with God all things are possible.
Matthew 19:26

Jesus said, "With God all things are possible." To me, that means then that nothing is hopeless. Only when a person has been blinded to the truth of hope in God can hopelessness take hold in one's heart and mind. God does not believe in hopelessness, and neither should you. It's a word that can kill without firing a shot. It's poison to the spirit. The antidote for hopelessness is truth.

Be sure you read that truth correctly and completely. It states:

With God, nothing is hopeless

In our limited, human realm of thought, many things appear to be hopeless. However, in this book, I'm talking about the all-encompassing truth of God. God looks at everything from His limitless, infinite perspective. God knows no boundaries and no impossibilities. Conversely, we think within the limitation of three-dimensional space and time. In our self-confined thinking, we've determined that there are very definite limits regarding what is possible and what is not, what we can reasonably hope for and what we cannot.

Whether or not you are a student of the Bible, you've most likely heard the story of Moses and the parting of the Red Sea. If ever there appeared to be a hopeless situation, that was one. The children of Israel, slaves of the Egyptians, had recently been freed by Pharaoh when he finally succumbed after God had inflicted a series of plagues on Egypt. A few days after Pharaoh freed the slaves, he had a change of heart and sent his army out to murder his former slaves. Unfortunately for the Israelites, they had camped on the edge of the Red Sea. They were backed up against the water, with no way of escape. Pharaoh's soldiers were highly trained and well armed. The Israelites were tired and hungry. They had neither weapons nor combat training. They were trapped and about to be annihilated. Their situation certainly appeared to be hopeless. But was it really? No, not to God. For God, it was surprisingly simple. Do you remember what happened? I love this story. God caused the waters of the Red Sea to part, leaving a path of dry land right through the middle of the seabed. Then, He sent down a pillar of fire to block the advance of the Egyptian army. While the fire held the soldiers back, the Israelites crossed between the waters over to the other side of the sea. Then, as the last of the Israelites crossed the seabed, God removed the column of fire from in front of the Egyptian army. Thinking they were clear to resume their mission, the soldiers charged down into the seabed in renewed pursuit of the Israelites. When the Egyptian army was in the middle of the seabed, and apparently just moments from reaching their intended victims, God released the waters of the sea to flood back in. The entire Egyptian army was drowned, and God's people were safe and free at last. I'll repeat the truth:

With God, *nothing* is hopeless.

We must cling to hope no matter how things may seem at the moment. You can maintain your hope by having faith—faith in your God who loves you. Do you recall the verse about abiding in faith, hope, and love? Those three were linked together for a reason. Faith gives us hope. And we have hope because we know that God loves us and cares for us.

> Therefore humble yourselves under the mighty hand
> of God, that He may exalt you in due time, casting
> all your care upon Him, for He cares for you
> 1 Peter 5:6-8

We've all been in tough situations, sometimes even seemingly hopeless ones. But if you're reading this, then you survived your situation. By definition then, it wasn't hopeless, was it? You've heard the expression, "Whatever doesn't kill us makes us stronger." Our parents have told us we can learn from our problems. Actually, they were speaking greater truth than they may have realized. Consider these words from the Bible:

> we have access by faith into this grace in which we stand,
> and rejoice in hope of the glory of God.
> And not only that, but we also glory in tribulations,
> knowing that tribulation produces perseverance;
> and perseverance, character;
> and character, hope. Now hope does not disappoint,

because the love of God has been poured out in our hearts
by the Holy Spirit who was given to us.
Romans 5:2-5

When we encounter troubles, we can be hopeful and thankful—hopeful because we know God is there with us—His rod and His staff are comforting us—and thankful because God is giving us an opportunity to grow in our faith and become stronger to meet the next challenge in our lives, for it will surely come.

Sometimes, you may pray and it seems as if God doesn't hear you. Be assured, God hears every prayer. But know this: God is not a cosmic vending machine to just anyone who asks Him. He will answer the prayers only of those who believe in Him.

The Lord is far from the wicked,
But He hears the prayer of the righteous.
Proverbs 15:29

If you trust in, and love, God, He will be there for you. Just as a mother can pick out the cry of her child from among many, God knows the voices of His children.

The righteous cry out, and the Lord hears,
And delivers them out of all their troubles.
Psalm 34:17

Now this is the confidence that we have in Him,
that if we ask anything according to His will, He hears us.
1 John 5:14

If you don't get an answer to your prayers as quickly as you would like, don't confuse God's delay with His denial. God operates in His perfect timing, not ours. He has a reason for everything. Often, His reason for delaying a response is to afford us a learning experience. Jesus did just that when He delayed coming to the aid of His friends, Mary and Martha, the sisters of Lazarus. They had sent word to Jesus that Lazarus was quite ill, even to the point of death. Jesus understood the severity of the situation, and yet He delayed responding to their pleas for a few days. During that time, Jesus knew that Lazarus had died. Jesus intended to use the death of Lazarus as a teaching opportunity for His disciples and others. Let's pick up the story from John's gospel as Jesus has decided that it was time to go to see Mary and Martha.

When Jesus heard that, He said, "This sickness is not unto death, but for the glory of God, that the Son of God may be glorified through it." Now Jesus loved Martha and her sister and Lazarus. He stayed two more days in the place where He was. Then after this He said to the disciples, "Let us go to Judea again." ... "Our friend Lazarus sleeps, but I go that I may wake him up." Then His disciples said, "Lord, if he sleeps he will get well." However, Jesus spoke of his death, but they thought that He was speaking about taking rest in sleep. Then Jesus said to them plainly, "Lazarus is dead. And I am glad for your sakes that I was not there, that you may believe." ... So when Jesus came, He found that he had already been in the tomb four days ... Now Martha said to Jesus, "Lord, if You had been here, my brother would not have died. But even now I know that whatever You ask of God, God will give You." Jesus said to her, "Your brother will rise again." Martha said to Him, "I know that he will rise again in the resurrection at the last day." Jesus said to her, "I am the resurrection and the life. He who believes in Me, though he may die, he shall live. And whoever lives and believes in Me shall never die. Do you believe this?" She said to Him, "Yes, Lord, I believe that You are the Christ, the Son of God, who is to come into the world." ... Then, when Mary came where Jesus was, and saw Him, she fell down at His feet, saying to Him, "Lord, if You had been here, my brother would not have died." … And He said, "Where have you laid him?" They said to Him, "Lord, come and see." … Then the Jews said … "Could not this Man, who opened the eyes of the blind, also have kept this man from dying?" Then Jesus … came to the tomb. Jesus said, "Take away the stone." Martha, the sister of him who was dead, said to Him, "Lord, by this time there is a stench, for he has been dead four days." Jesus said to her, "Did I not say to you that if you would believe you would see the glory of God?" Then they took away the stone … and Jesus lifted up His eyes and said, "Father, I thank You that You have heard Me. And I know that You always hear Me, but because of the people who are standing by I said this, that they may believe that You sent Me." … He cried with a loud voice, "Lazarus, come forth!" And he who had died came out bound hand and foot with grave clothes, and his face was wrapped with a cloth. Jesus said to them, "Loose him, and let him go."

John 11:4-44

Even earthly death is not hopeless if it's God's will to change it. Jesus delayed His response to the prayers of His friends Mary and Martha for a very good reason. If you have been praying for something, keep your faith and hold onto hope. God is waiting for the right time and circumstance to give you His answer. He has the eternal picture in mind. You and I can only see what's going on right here and now. You don't know His plan for your future. But you can be assured, He has one. Here is the truth again.

For I know the plans I have for you," declares the LORD, "plans to prosper you, ………plans to give you hope and a future.

Jeremiah 29:11

Trust in Him always, and believe that He will do what is best for you every time, all the time. Don't restrict your expectation of His capability; there is no limit to what God can do for you. Remember Jesus' words.

With men this is impossible, but with God all things are possible
Matthew 19:26

If we know the truth, we can be hopeful rather than hopeless. With our understanding of God's truth comes this hope-filled knowledge:

And we know that all things work together
for good to those who love God,
to those who are the called according to His purpose.
Romans 8:28

When your situation is looking bleak, when troubles seem to be overwhelming, when things appear to be getting out of control, you can have hope in the fact that the greatest power in the universe is with you. When you partner with God, nothing and no one can stop you.

What then shall we say to these things?
If God is for us, who can be against us?
Romans 8:31

If you are wondering whether or not you can overcome an obstacle that you are facing, listen to this next truth and then you'll wonder no more.

Yet in all these things we are more than
conquerors through Him who loved us.
Romans 8:37

Paul, who had a very personal encounter with Jesus, just told you that when you have Christ in you, you are more than a conqueror. It seems to me that you stand in a pretty strong position and have good reason to be hopeful. God has given you in writing what you need to know to be hopeful in all things. You simply need to go into His word and read His words of hope:

> For whatever things were written before,
> were written for our learning,
> that we through the patience and comfort
> of the Scriptures might have hope.
> Romans 15:4

Trials, tribulations, disappointments, sorrows, and losses are inevitably going to occur in your life, in my life, in all of our lives. That's just the way it is; that's life. But thankfully, we have a wonderful, loving Father who is always there to comfort us and see us through whatever challenge we may be facing. We will never be alone with our troubles. God has given us His word on that—the Bible. I pray you will use that valuable resource, especially when your hope is fading and you need encouragement. If you've not been a Bible reader, please take some time and take a look into the word of God. Ask God to open your eyes to truths that pertain to your life right now. You'll be amazed where He leads you. And you'll be grateful for what He speaks to you through those words.

I want to end this chapter with a verse that serves as a hope-filled benediction.

> Now may the God of hope fill you with
> all joy and peace in believing,
> that you may abound in hope by the power of the Holy Spirit.
> Romans 15:13

✝

PEACE

Beyond Our Understanding

When I speak of the peace of God, I'm not talking about the absence of war. God's peace is, as our friendly wizard from Oz says, a horse of a different color. Consider these words from the Bible:

Be anxious for nothing,
but in everything by prayer and supplication, with thanksgiving,
let your requests be known to God;
and the peace of God which surpasses all understanding,
will guard your hearts and minds through Christ Jesus
Philippians 4:6-7

Did you catch the key words *"which surpasses all understanding"*? The peace of God is beyond what you or I can imagine or comprehend. What it means to you is that no matter what situation you may find yourself in, the world may actually be coming to an end, yet you can be at peace in your heart and mind. Why is peace important? That's easy. Remember the last time you were stressed out about something? Did you enjoy that feeling? That's why peace is important. When your mind is in a state of unrest, you are less effective in your thinking, your decision making is hindered, you feel uncomfortable, and you certainly can't be peaceful. A mind disturbed is a mind in trouble. Mental unrest is one of the most undesirable states of human existence. Almost as desperately as we desire love, we need peace. Love may be the key to our existence, but peace is what enables us to enjoy our existence. Peace is the state of mind in which God intended for us to live. When you have peace, you can, as Kipling said, "Keep your head when all about you are losing theirs." The peace of God will allow you to rest in the assurance that when your life is in God's hands, He will see you through any circumstance—all the way until you leave this world, and you stand in His presence.

In the above verse, God has told you that whenever you are in need, or in trouble, or are simply fearful or confused in a situation, you can call on Him and He will take care of you and give you peace while He's doing it. Is that not the recipe for the end of stress in your life? I didn't say the end of problems in your life; you will always have those from time to time. But you need not be anxious about them. With God's peace in your heart, you can handle all your problems calmly and confidently. Of course, it's easy for me to say that, but it's true nonetheless. It will take time to develop the confidence in God that will give you that degree of peace. As you progress in the renewing of your mind, your peace will grow.

God's peace is without and within. It's *inter*personal, and *intra*personal. Personal peace must precede relational peace. Peace begins with ourselves. We cannot know peace with our brother if we don't know peace within ourselves. That is why you must renew your mind with the truth of God. As you increase in your understanding of God's truth, your thoughts will shift from anxiety and concern to calmness and peace. Paul wrote:

let the peace of God rule in your hearts ... and be thankful.
Colossians 3:15

Once we establish peace within ourselves, then we can:

Pursue peace with all people
Hebrews 12:14

Once again, I am smiling as I'm writing and thinking about this. God knows exactly what we need at all times. That's why He taught us about so many things in His word. He wanted to be sure He covered everything that we would need to enjoy our lives and live happily and successfully.

When you don't have peace, every aspect of your life can be affected. You become unable to concentrate on necessary tasks such as your work, your relationships will certainly be affected, you lose patience with others more quickly, you can't sleep, and even your health can become affected. Lack of peace can kill you. Worry and stress are deadlier than bullets. A bullet may only wound a part of you. Stress affects all of you. Stroke, heart attack, high blood pressure—all those things are results of a lack of peace. Lack of peace results in dis-ease, mentally and physically. Here's a great verse from the book of Proverbs. It talks about how living according to God's rules will benefit you now and in your future.

But let your heart keep my commands;
For length of days and long life
And peace they will add to you.
Proverbs 3:1-2

God had a good reason for telling us to "let the peace of God rule in your hearts" and "pursue peace with all people." He knows that without peace, we are in trouble, possibly grave trouble—the kind of trouble that can actually lead us to our grave.

The only way to have real, satisfying inner and outer peace is by spending time with God and getting to know Him and His truth. Isaiah was inspired by God to write this truth for us for us regarding God's plan for us to have peace:

> You will keep him in perfect peace, whose mind is stayed on You
> Isaiah 26:3

Keep your mind *on* God and He will keep your mind *in* peace. I hope that by now, you're seeing that God just wants to love you and give you a wonderful life. He wants to give you blessings and take care of you, and He wants to be sure your mind is happy and at peace. He cares for everything about you, and He will take care of every part of you.

Peace is one of the most desirable characteristics that man can possess. Peaceful men command the respect of other men. In a time of crisis, they are an island of sanity in the sea of confusion and chaos. We are drawn to them by their peace. They give us a much-needed sense of security and reassurance. Of course, the greatest example of a peaceful man was Jesus Christ. He taught ideas that almost seem impossible, and yet when contemplated, they make perfect sense. During a teaching session, Jesus made just such a statement.

> To him who strikes you on the one cheek, offer the other also.
> Luke 6:29

At first glance, that statement seems absurd. But Jesus understood that nothing is to be gained by answering violence with violence. When all involved are engaged in conflict, the prospect of peace is impossible. The only result that can be had is one of destruction and further separation. Peace and reconciliation can only occur when at least one of the parties is willing to rise above the instinct for violence and let his power of reason prevail. We must allow peace to be the order of the day, or the day will be lost. We cannot continue to exist without peace. Peace enables us to maintain the hope of our future. In the absence of peace, we can only wait for our inevitable demise. By definition, the absence of peace is conflict, and conflict breeds death and destruction. Whether it's the death of a relationship or a nation, its cause can be traced back to a lack of peace.

> Peace I leave with you, My peace I give to you;
> not as the world gives do I give to you.
> Let not your heart be troubled, neither let it be afraid.
> John 14:27

Peace and love are the only hope for mankind's continued coexistence with himself. Jesus taught us peace for that very reason. He had to remind us of the obvious quite often. Intellectually, we know that we can only live by peace, for without it, we die. But since we are emotional beings, we act as such and in so doing, we frequently create for ourselves a lack of peace. Then we complain when we suffer the consequences. Jesus must have felt as though He was talking to a pile of bricks sometimes. On one occasion, He even expressed His exasperation with us.

> O faithless and perverse generation, how long shall I be with you?
> How long shall I bear with you?
> Matthew 17:17

I have to laugh when I read that verse. Here was God incarnate, trying to cope with the pinnacle of His creation—humans, with all of our limitations and faults. Jesus spent every minute of His time here on earth loving and teaching people, and yet they continued to ignore Him and reject His teaching. I occasionally wonder if He ever questioned Himself about His own decision to create us. I can imagine Him shaking His head in disbelief at us sometimes ... kind of like we do with our own children. I guess we deserve it. He made us, and we made our children. For the most part we even wanted them. Remember the caution I cited in my introduction? Be careful what you ask for ... Our children are God's payback.

As you work to achieve your personal peace, you will find that it is an all-encompassing state of being. Peace involves the attributes of godliness that we've been discussing—love, forgiveness, grace, and mercy, as well as many others. After all, it surpasses our understanding. In fact, we may never completely grasp the entire meaning of peace. But thankfully, we don't have to understand it; we can just give thanks and accept it as a wonderful gift from God for our benefit. Here's a nice little teaser for you—living in peace here on earth gives us a glimpse of what lies ahead for us if we choose to accept salvation through Jesus, God's Son.

> ... for the kingdom of God is
> ... righteousness and peace and joy in the Holy Spirit.
> Romans 14:17

That sounds like something worth looking into. We will, in the next chapter. But for now, I'll end this chapter with words that biblical writers commonly used to end their writings.

> Now may the God of hope fill you with
> all joy and peace in believing,
> that you may abound in hope by the power of the Holy Spirit.
> Romans 15:13

†

JOY

An Inexpressible State of Mind

went to dictionary.com for a definition of "joy." Unfortunately, all I got was the worldly definition—the emotion of great delight or happiness.

That sounds reasonable enough, but I'm not talking about worldly truth in this book, I'm talking about God's truth. So that definition won't do.

In the realm of God's truth, Joy is a little more difficult to define. It's a state of mind that transcends happiness and delightfulness. Joy gives you a deep sense of contentment and security. In fact, you can be filled with joy even in a moment of unhappiness.

Happiness is transient; it depends on the moment. Joy is deeper; it is independent of the moment. Joy comes from within us. Happiness results from circumstances outside of us. It's fun to be happy, it feels good. But it's satisfying to be joyful. A compliment from a friend can make you happy, but the love of a child brings you joy.

Why am I talking about joy in a book about truth that can help you with your life? Here's why. Joy is a truth of God. It is a gift that He can instill in your heart. The joy that God gives you changes your entire perspective about yourself, your life, and the world around you. When you look from the vantage point of joy, you see that everything is under God's control, and therefore okay. You see problems as just things that you must handle. They no longer appear as insurmountable obstacles that can stop you. With the joy of the Lord in your heart, you are an irresistible force, and all formerly immovable objects become movable. Joy keeps you feeling strong through times when you might otherwise feel weak and unable to endure.

for the joy of the Lord is your strength
Nehemiah 8:10

When you find yourself in the middle of a crisis or problem of some sort, you may feel weak, confused, worried, or unsure of many things. It's then that the joy of the Lord will be your strength. When all else seems to be failing, the calmness and assurance of the joy of the Lord gives you strength. I was recently told of an elderly woman who had numerous health problems as she neared the end of her life. But, as her daughter related to me, this woman always seemed to be calm, peaceful, confident and happy. Her daughter also told me that her mother had a strong relationship with the Lord. That explained it all to me. Her mother had the joy of the Lord in her heart. All her earthly physical problems and pain were just stuff she was going through. Her mind was secure in the joy of her Lord.

You will keep him in perfect peace, Whose mind is stayed on You,
Because he trusts in You.
Isaiah 26:3

Be of good comfort, be of one mind, live in peace;
and the God of love and peace will be with you
2 Corinthians 13:11

That dear, sweet woman knew and loved her Lord, and He blessed her with His joy during her time of sickness and suffering. When her family was sad and struggling, her joy was light and encouragement to them. The joy of the Lord was truly her strength!

If you have joy, true joy, the joy of the Lord, in your heart, you will be much more effective in everything you do. Without joy, worry and insecurity can cloud your mind and interfere with your discernment and decision making. Joy gives you the peace of mind that allows you clarity of thinking. With joy, you possess the knowledge that nothing can happen that you can't handle. You will have an unshakeable confidence and assurance that you have the ability to withstand any and all challenges and problems that may occur in your life. When you have joy, you will be kinder and more loving toward others. You can't help it; that's just what happens when the joyful Spirit of the Lord is operating inside you.

When trouble strikes, you can have an unhappy experience and still be joyful. The unhappy event will pass, but your knowledge of who you are in the Lord will never change. That is joy.

If you don't feel that you now have the joy of the Lord, but you desire to have it, ask God, and He will be faithful to give it to you.

Ask, and you will receive, that your joy may be full.
John 16:24

Jesus said:

These things I have spoken to you, that My joy may remain in you
John 15:11

God knows how important His joy is to you. It brings a whole new dimension of enjoyment to your life. Maybe that's why "joy" is in the middle of the word enjoyment. God wants it to be in the middle of your life as well.

But let all those rejoice who put their trust in You; Let them ever
shout for joy, because You defend them;
Let those also who love Your name
Be joyful in You.
For You, O LORD, will bless the righteous;
With favor You will surround him as with a shield.
Psalm 5:11-12

I'll end this brief chapter with a line from one of John's letters. He was talking about writing to encourage people. I too am writing to offer you encouragement in your life. Seek the joy of the Lord; you'll be glad you did.

And these things we write to you that your joy may be full.
1 John 1:4

✝

GRACE AND MERCY

A pretty good deal

Grace

Dictionary.com defines it as:

the freely given, unmerited favor and love of God.
the influence or spirit of God operating in humans to regenerate or strengthen them. virtue or excellence of divine origin.

In my words, Grace is God giving us what we *don't* deserve.

Mercy

Dictionary.com defines it as:

compassionate or kindly forbearance shown toward an offender
the disposition to be compassionate or forbearing
the discretionary power to pardon someone or to mitigate punishment.

In my words, Mercy is God *not* giving us what we *do* deserve

Yes, I'd call that a pretty good deal, a couple of them, actually. I hope you recognize Grace and Mercy as further evidence of God's love for you. He certainly did not have to give us either of those great gifts. He simply wanted to, because He loves us.

> I thank my God always concerning you for the grace of God
> which was given to you by Christ Jesus
> 1 Corinthians 1:4

I shudder to think of our lives without the grace of God. "There but for the grace of God, go I." We use that expression when we are thinking of someone less fortunate than ourselves. Well, without the wonderful gift of God's grace, we'd all be less fortunate than we are now.

> But to each one of us grace was given
> according to the measure of Christ's gift
> Ephesians 4:7

Have you ever stopped and taken the time to give thanks to God for His gift of grace? If not, perhaps you should. He certainly deserves our heartfelt thanks. I know I owe Him untold gratitude—for a million reasons, most notably, my recent accident. By all accounts, God was more than gracious in granting me the outcome I enjoyed. I use the term enjoyed in the grateful sense. Few people are hit broadside at ninety-six mph and not only live to tell about it, but are in reasonably good shape. I'll take my scar and my pain any day in lieu of death or paralysis or brain damage (some may argue I received plenty) that I might have suffered.

> God is able to make all grace abound toward you,
> that you, always having all sufficiency in all things,
> may have an abundance for every good work.
> 2 Corinthians 9:8

And He said to me, "My grace is sufficient for you"
2 Corinthians 12:9

As God has given to us, we should give back to others. God did unto us; let's do unto others. We'll all be better for it if we will offer grace and love to one another. Being kind really isn't that difficult when you realize that others deep inside are really no different than yourself. We're all just people who want to be loved, and for the most part, we're all doing the best we can with who and what we are. We've all got issues, we're all imperfect, and we've all fallen short in some way. In the words of a popular song from some years back, we all need to "try a little tenderness."

For there is no difference; for all have sinned
and fall short of the glory of God,
being justified freely by His grace through the
redemption that is in Christ Jesus.
Romans 3:22-24

Being imperfect ourselves, we have no right to judge others. Rather than condemn and criticize, we must learn to encourage and help. We mustn't forget that we will all reap as we've sown. If we want to receive God's grace, we must begin by offering others our grace. Remember, there are eternal consequences for our choices and actions in this life.

When you consider the reality of the consequences of not accepting God's gift of salvation through His grace, you'll appreciate how truly great His grace is toward you. Without the grace of God, we'd all be lost for eternity—a fate that is actually worse than death!

Cast into the lake of fire and brimstone where
the beast and the false prophet are.

And they will be tormented day and night
forever and ever. This is the second death
Revelation 20:10,14

For the wages of sin is death,
but the gift of God is eternal life in Christ Jesus our Lord.
Romans 6:23

I've talked to many people who say they don't believe that: 1. Jesus is the only way to eternity in Heaven and 2. Without salvation through Jesus, we are doomed to eternity in Hell. Let me just say that in this case, ignorance is not bliss. What you don't know *can* and *will* hurt you. I discussed salvation and eternity in the "It's All About Jesus" chapter. For now, consider this next verse and open your hearts to the truth therein. It is absolutely essential for you to understand and appreciate that all you have, all you are, and all you ever will be is due solely to the sublime, loving grace of God.

But God, who is rich in mercy, because of His
great love with which He loved us,
even when we were dead in trespasses, made
us alive together with Christ
For by grace you have been saved through faith,
and that not of yourselves; it is the gift of God,
Ephesians 2:8

The gift of God, the awesome, matchless gift of God, is His grace that saves us. No matter how many birthdays you live through, no matter how many Christmases you experience, you can never,

ever receive a gift like God's gift of salvation. It doesn't get any better than that.

When you choose to accept God's gift, you will bring Him untold joy. I dare say that nothing brings more happiness to the heart of God than for one of His children to recognize His truth and to choose to live in that truth. In fact, all of heaven rejoices when you accept His gift of salvation.

> Likewise, I say to you, there is joy in the
> presence of the angels of God
> over one sinner who repents. (and comes
> to salvation) - parenthesis mine
> Luke 15:10

There is rejoicing in heaven because, as we will see in a later chapter, our salvation is the bottom line to our existence. It's why God made us in the first place, so we could spend eternity in heaven with Him.

So, Grace is God giving us what we don't deserve—His love and His blessings.

Now, let's look at Mercy, which as I said at the beginning of this chapter is God not giving us what we do deserve—punishment for our sins and for some of us, rejecting Him.

A good place to start our discussion of Mercy is with this next verse.

> Have mercy on me, O Lord, for I am weak
> Psalm 6:2

That simple verse may sum up our entire existence as it relates to us and God. We are weak in spirit, willpower, wisdom, morality, and faith when compared to the standards of God. There has only been one person who has ever measured up—Jesus Christ. All the rest of us fall short. We need the strength of God more than we could ever know. People who say they don't need God are deluding themselves. That may be a pretty blunt statement, but it's true nonetheless. We especially need God's mercy precisely because of our weakness in the areas I mentioned above. Our erroneous ways are exposed by the light of God's truth. Without His mercy, our lives and our deeds would earn us a quick trip to the wrong side of judgment. We cannot live godly lives without God's help. It's just that simple.

Yes, I know that many people have lived "successful" lives without ever paying any attention to God. But their lives are successful according to human terms as related to this life here on earth. In reality, if they've chosen to live without God in their lives, then as their lives relate to eternity, they were utter failures. All their earthly success means absolutely nothing the moment they draw their last breath. As the saying goes, you can't take it with you. All that "success" is worthless to God if it wasn't lived for Him, with Him, and through Him. In the big picture of the truth of God and eternity, it was all a waste of time.

> But what things were gain to me, these
> I have counted loss for Christ.
> Yet indeed I also count all things loss for the excellence
> of the knowledge of Christ Jesus my Lord, for
> whom I have suffered the loss of all things,
> and count them as rubbish, that I may gain Christ
> Philippians 3:6-8

The writer of that verse, the Apostle Paul, had in fact lived a very "successful" life in earthly terms—that is, until he had a personal encounter with the Truth on the road to Damascus. Up until that time, Paul had used his success and his position to gain authority to persecute Christians. He was apparently quite brutal. But God, in His wisdom and His mercy, decided to use Paul's gifts as a leader and an influential speaker for good. Rather than punish Paul for tormenting Christ's followers, God showed him mercy. As a result, Paul quickly and clearly learned that all he had was "rubbish" if he didn't repent and accept God's gift of salvation, and dedicate his life to serving God as an ambassador of the truth.

I don't know if you are familiar with the story, but Jesus caused Paul to be blind for three days until he was able to "see" the truth. Then Jesus opened Paul's eyes so that Paul could then live a genuinely successful life in service to God. After Paul regained his sight, he was able for the first time to see the truth of his life because his vision was now illuminated by the "Light of the World." Paul became one of God's greatest preachers and teachers.

I share Paul's story because I want you to understand that God can and will use anyone who is willing to serve Him. David, the "man after God's own heart," had a man killed so David could have the man's wife. I bet you haven't done that. So, don't worry if your past hasn't been a good one. God forgives and "remembers no more." When you repent and surrender to God, you start with a clean slate. That is the mercy of God. With God, it truly is never too late. God searches your heart, and if it's right *with* Him, it's right *for* Him.

Let me remind you that you don't have to give up your job and go into the ministry to serve Him. You can serve Him right where you are, as you are. When you accept His gracious gift, through His mercy, He will transform you, so that you will begin living as an example of His grace and mercy.

> Let your light so shine before men,
> that they may see your good works and
> glorify your Father in heaven.
> Matthew 5:16

When you walk in the grace of God's mercy, you will be a light that shines in the darkness of the world around you, perhaps in your own home, in your workplace, where you play, or wherever you go. People will begin to notice that there is something different about you, and they will want whatever it is that you have. Trust me on that one. You will be holding the answer to what others are searching for, even if they don't know what "it" is. Sooner or later, they are going to come to you. I know, because that's what happened to me. During my first year of Chiropractic college, I felt an inexplicable need to talk to a particular man in one of my classes. He wasn't the type of man I would normally have befriended, but I had to talk to Him. Over the course of the semester, our conversations drifted to faith and God. I didn't realize it at the time, but what was happening was this - God was calling me and he used that man to witness to me. God, in His perfect timing, knew that I was ready to receive His truth in my life. That's how He works sometimes, you don't see Him coming, but suddenly, there He is! So don't be surprised when he puts someone on your heart; there is a reason.

When you are in need, when you're at the end of your own resources and strength, call on God and ask Him to have mercy on you and your situation. He has proven that He is merciful and He will come to your aid in your time of need. When you ask, have faith and believe.

When Jesus departed from there, two blind men followed Him,
crying out and saying, "Son of David, have mercy on us!"
And when He had come into the house,
the blind men came to Him.
And Jesus said to them, "Do you believe that
I am able to do this?" They said to Him, "Yes,
Lord." Then He touched their eyes, saying,
"According to your faith let it be to you."
And their eyes were opened.
Matthew 9:27-30

For as you were once disobedient to God,
yet have now obtained mercy
... even so these also have now been disobedient,
that through the mercy shown you they also may obtain mercy.
Romans 11:30-31

God's mercy toward us comes in many forms. Sometimes it's
as healing, other times it's as forgiveness. Sometimes, it's as a gift
of some sort. But however it's given, it's always undeserved—that's
Grace. Grace unto Mercy, Mercy out of Grace. We will never fully
understand God's gifts to us; they are unfathomable. Within the
realm of our own limitations, we enjoy the unlimited favor of God.
We can only give inadequate thanks and be grateful that He loves
the unlovable, and He saves the undeserving. By His Grace, His
Mercy truly endures forever

†

SIN, SATAN AND HELL

Deadly and Determined

Up until now, I've been talking about the good things, the positive side of our existence—God and Jesus and goodness and light. But if there is a good side, then there must, by definition, be a bad side. Unfortunately, now I must talk about darkness and evil. I don't like thinking about Satan and evil. I don't particularly want to write about him either. I don't like to put these thoughts in my mind, or yours. Why then am I writing this? I must if I am going to be faithful in presenting God's truth to you. The devil, Satan, is very real, and he is devoted to destroying you and me. If I don't warn you about the reality of him and the threat he poses to you, then I am guilty of leaving you defenseless in the battle for your life, both now and for eternity. I want to be sure that you understand the truth about evil and what it means to you and everyone else, including those you love.

The Bible warns us to be aware and wary of the devil.

Be sober, be vigilant;
because your adversary the devil walks about like a roaring lion,
seeking whom he may devour.
1 Peter 5:8

You might reasonably ask, "Can't I just ignore the devil, and stay away from evil things?" No. If Satan were passive and only bothered you when you went into his yard, for example, then I'd say, "Yes, just leave him alone and you'll be fine," just as you'll be okay if you leave a sleeping dog alone, or don't try to take his food from him while he's eating, and that sort of thing. But the devil is anything but passive, as the verse above points out.

You see, Satan knows that his time is limited. He knows he has to act now, or his opportunity will pass. How does he know his time is limited? I don't want to devote a lot of time to the devil's history, but briefly, I'll tell you a little background. Originally, Satan was known as Lucifer. He was one of the most beautiful and powerful and highly esteemed of all the angels in heaven. But he was also prideful, and he let his pride overcome his love for God, his Creator. Lucifer decided that he should be equal to God. Remember the old saying "pride comes before the fall"? This is where it came from. God would not tolerate Lucifer's arrogance, and He threw Lucifer out of heaven. As a result of his punishment, Lucifer was determined to wage war with God, thinking that he could defeat God and take His place. Lucifer persuaded one third of the angels to follow him, promising them all sorts of privileges in the new kingdom he was going to create. Thus Hell and demons were born. Lucifer became Satan, and the war was on.

Satan knows that in the end, he loses and will be cast into the lake of fire and he will burn for eternity. As you can imagine, because he knows that, he is full of hate and evil intentions and has set as his purpose to destroy as many souls as possible and take them with him into eternal damnation.

A lot of people think that's just a fairy tale and the devil isn't really real and we'll all just go happily to heaven when it's all said and done. That right there is the greatest lie of the devil. That is why he is so dangerous. He puts that thought in people's minds so they will downplay the threat and just go on living any way they want, believing that when they die, all will be well.

If that were true, then the entirety of Jesus' life and mission would have been unnecessary. But it's not true. The devil is real, hell is real, and that is precisely why Jesus came and did what He did to save us from all that.

Right now, I want to try to convince you to take Satan and evil seriously. He is deadly serious. Satan is pure evil. There is no limit to how heinous an act he will commit when given the opportunity. You cannot overestimate him, and please, don't underestimate him. Try to think of the worst possible thing you can imagine, and you won't even be halfway to his level of evil. Satan has the ability to put evil thoughts into the heart and mind of anyone who doesn't know the Lord and doesn't know how to resist his ploys.

How can you protect yourself from him? Knowing the truth of God will protect you from Satan's influence. In fact, Scripture tells us that when we have the Lord in our hearts, we will have the power to defeat Satan when he approaches us.

He who is in you is greater than he who is in the world.
1 John 4:4

If Satan does try to tempt you in some way, just stand up to him and say no. Jesus is more powerful than Satan. If you have Christ in you, then you have His strength in you, and Satan cannot stand up to you.

Resist the devil and he will flee from you
James 4:7

If you doubt the reality of evil, then for just a moment, consider a child molester. Do you really believe that a man, of and by himself, could do such a thing as to rape and torture and kill a precious little two-year-old child? Even criminals know that is off limits. It's well documented what happens to child molesters if they are put into the general population of a prison. They get killed in brutal fashion in short order. Nobody tolerates the offense of harming a child. So how does it happen? Something, some very evil influence got into that person in order for him to have been able to commit such an act of unimaginable cruelty. Only Satan, the prince of darkness, could conceive of and carry out a deed so evil.

You've probably heard Christians say that there is no in between. Either you're with God or you're with Satan. That sounds kind of extreme, doesn't it? That's what I thought. You may say, "Can't I be neutral? I just want to be a good person. I don't want to be a Jesus freak. It's not like I'm going out raping and killing." Well, let's see what God says about neutrality.

I know your works, that you are neither cold nor
hot … So then, because you are lukewarm,
and neither cold nor hot, I will vomit you out of My mouth.
Revelation 3:15-22

God is serious about your decision to be with Him or not. Remember who is talking here. Those are the words of God, the Creator of everything that exists. He made it all, good and evil. He knows that there is no in between. You are either in God's camp or the enemy's camp. If you are not clearly with God, then you are against Him.

Jesus said it as plainly as it can be said:

> He who is not with Me is against Me……..
> Matthew 12:23

Those are strong words indeed. You may not be a Satan worshiper, or you may not be going out and actively and intentionally trying to sin, but if you have not consciously chosen to be with God, then you are, in fact, against Him.

Dear reader, please understand, I'm just the messenger here. I didn't and don't make the rules. I'm just sharing the truth with you, because I don't want you to be deceived into thinking that you can get by on your own with no risk of trouble, condemnation, or judgment. Eventually, we will all stand before God and give an accounting of ourselves. You cannot ignore God and live as you please and then expect that when you face Him in eternity, He will suddenly say "Howdy partner, come on in!" Here is the truth, in Jesus' own words, of what will happen if you try to live without the Lord.

> Not everyone who says to Me, 'Lord, Lord,'
> shall enter the kingdom of heaven,
> … I will declare to them,
> 'I never knew you; depart from Me, you who practice lawlessness!'
> Matthew 7:21-23

That certainly puts each of us in a spot, doesn't it? You've got to decide, and make your choice. Please realize that your life is not a game. You are playing for very high, eternal stakes. You are here for a reason, and a lot of that reason is to decide where you want to spend your eternal life after you leave this one here on earth.

If you still think that you can get by with your own ideas and live according to your own way and will, listen to the words that Jesus spoke later in the same passage as the verse above.

Either make the tree good and its fruit good,
or else make the tree bad and its fruit bad; for
a tree is known by its fruit………..
For out of the abundance of the heart the mouth speaks…………
But I say to you that for every idle word men may
speak, they will give account of it in the day of
judgment. For by your words you will be justified,
and by your words you will be condemned."
Matthew 12:33-37

Wow Geoff, you started this book out sounding friendly and helpful. Now you sound like one of those intolerant, hell-fire and brimstone preachers. Dear reader, I'm still me, the friendly and helpful guy. But this book is about the truth of God. I can't just pick out the fun stuff and give that to you and dismiss the bottom line. I'm writing this out of love, with a desire to share all of God's truth with you. Therefore I will tell you the truth, the whole truth, and nothing but the truth.

I'm writing this book because I want to be sure that you and I can meet one day in eternity. And like it or not, these truths are in God's word. We have to deal with them. I'd rather present them to you now and risk you being upset with me but at least having the knowledge of the truth. The alternative would be for me to keep this as a happy, feel good book and let you be blindsided on the day of judgment. At least now you've been exposed to God's truth and you can make your own decision. I feel that I owe it to you to tell you the truth because I stated in my introduction that I was writing about God's truth. From this point forward, what you do with it is up to you.

God knows that evil and sin are real, and that whether we like it or not, or believe it or not, we are sinners. And as such, without Him, we will fall short and end up separated from Him forever.

> But God demonstrates His own love toward us,
> in that while we were still sinners, Christ died for us.
> Romans 5:8

God is still friendly and loving too. In fact, if you realize the order of things, you will begin to appreciate just how loving God is toward you and me. Note the words: "While we were still sinners." God didn't say to you, "Okay, you be good and *then* I'll save you." He offered Himself and salvation to you first, before you even existed. Now it's up to you to accept it. Try getting a deal like that anywhere else. His offer to save you from the consequences of your sins is not performance based. You don't have to earn it. In fact, you cannot earn it.

> For by grace you have been saved through faith,
> and that not of yourselves; it is the gift of God,
> not of works, lest anyone should boast
> Ephesians 2:8-9

God offered you life in eternity with Him for one very simple reason—He loves you, and He wants to spend time with you. That's all there is to it. He only asks that you accept Him as your God, Jesus as your Savior, and that you make at least a reasonable effort to live by His principles of love and truth. He doesn't expect you to be perfect, or even close. He knows none of us can do that.

> for all have sinned and fall short of the glory of God,
> Romans 3:23

Remember the classic verse that you've heard many times.

For God so loved the world that He gave His only begotten Son,
that whoever believes in Him should not
perish but have everlasting life.
John 3:16

God knows sin and Satan are real and dangerous. That is why so much of the Bible is dedicated to a discussion of sin and its consequences. Sin is the reason God sent Jesus, His Son, to earth to save us. If the threat of sin is such a real concern to God, don't you think you ought to give it some thought yourself? I'm trying to find a way to present this without sounding preachy, but it is what it is. This is truly a matter of life and death. Consider Jesus' words on the subject of sin and repentance.

unless you repent you will all likewise perish.
Luke 13:3

That statement leaves no room for negotiation. A thought just occurred to me. Would Jesus have gone through the miserable torture and death that He endured if this issue of sin and death weren't extremely serious? I'm sure He could have found a better way to spend a Friday afternoon. He gave everything He had—His own life—to save us from the consequences of our sins. If nothing else, we owe it to Him to at least take a long, hard look at the whole idea.

Once you appreciate the reality of sin, and then you think about what Jesus did to save you from eternal misery in Hell, you will gain a new perspective on Jesus—who He is and how much He loves you. And when you begin to see love from that perspective, your own ability to love will change and grow in a wonderful way. You may for the first time in your life feel true, genuine love for yourself and others.

I hope that now you will start to think of yourself the way God thinks of you—as His precious child for whom He willingly gave His life. You are worth every bit of the love God gives you. Believe it, because it's the truth!

✝

YOU CAN CHANGE YOUR LIFE

It's Up To You

I f you're not satisfied with your life as it is now, you can change it. God will show you how, and then He'll help you do it. Actually, it will be the Holy Spirit working within you that will be making the changes. Neither you nor I can make these kinds of changes within ourselves. They are supernatural changes. They have to be supernatural, because our natural nature would not be willing to make these changes. We would cling selfishly and tenaciously to our old habits and desires. Change, even for the better, is usually scary and uncomfortable. We have to be willing to move out of our comfort zone and into the unknown. We must have trust and faith in the agent of our change - the Holy Spirit of God.

I can write these words and tell you that you can trust Him implicitly, but in the end, you must make that decision for yourself. You must want to change and be willing to trust in God. When you do, He will begin His work in you. You simply need to be willing to surrender yourself and accept His leading as you grow into the new you. Don't worry, you will still be you. You'll just have a new, softer, kinder, gentler, more understanding and compassionate heart.

Actually, you will quickly find out just how much you will still be you. When you accept the Lord into your life and ask Him to come into your heart, Satan becomes very angry. He mounts a furious attack on you and tries to tempt you by rousing up all your old sinful desires. He knows that if he doesn't break you down quickly, he'll lose you to Christ. Remember, Satan's goal is to destroy you. He doesn't want you to be saved and spend eternity in Heaven.

Many new Christians report struggling with a lot of temptation when they first become Christians. You must accept that as part of the deal. It happens to all of us. Even when established Christians take steps and grow in their Christian walk, they get hit with all manner of temptations. This is when we all must remember two verses that I quoted earlier.

Resist the devil and he will flee from you
James 4:7

He who is in you is greater than he who is in the world.
1 John 4:4

When you have the Holy Spirit, the Spirit of Christ, in you, you can overcome anything—if you truly want to overcome it. This is very important. I believe that ultimately when it comes right down to it, we all do what we truly want to do. If you give in to temptation, then that was more important to you than doing the thing that you knew to be right. At that point, your only hope is prayer. You must go to God and ask Him to remove the sinful desires from your heart and mind. Obviously you can't do it alone or you would have resisted the temptation in the first place. As you grow in the Lord, you will grow in respect for yourself. When you begin to realize the price God paid to save you—He sacrificed His beloved Son—you start to realize how valuable you are to God. When that happens, you begin to value yourself. I'm going to repeat a verse here to remind you of the price God paid for you and why He paid it.

For God so loved the world that He gave His only begotten Son,
that whoever believes in Him should not
perish but have everlasting life.
John 3:16

Think of it this way. If God saves you for eternity, then He must think you're pretty good, because now He's going to have to deal with you forever. If He didn't really love you, He'd just say, "See ya!" My point is this: if God thinks you're valuable and lovable, then you should think so too.

You must ask God to bring your mind back to the reality and assurance of His truth. It was during my time of trouble as I was praying in my distress at the lake house that God helped me realize that I didn't have to be in that state of mind. He showed me that I could change my mindset, my situation, and my life if I wanted to do so. I just needed to know the truth about how to do it. God put that truth in my mind. He will do the same for you, if you ask Him. He waits on all of us to call on Him with our needs and desires. If you need help with a problem in your life, or if you just need an answer to a question, or help with an important decision, talk to God. You can call on Him anytime. His helpline is open 24/7.

Amazing things happen when you ask God for help. He goes to work, and you can enjoy learning from Him, as I've done while writing this book. God revealed to me the truth that you **Can Change Your Life** by directing me to this verse:

> "......do not be conformed to this world,
> but be **transformed** by the **renewing** of your mind,
> that you may prove what is that good and
> acceptable and perfect will of God"
> Romans 12:2

You may be thinking "transformed into what?" That is a valid question. Before I try to answer that question, I'd like to share another verse with you. It's from Ezekiel, in the Old Testament. It was written about 571 BC. I tell you that because the content of this verse is consistent with verses of the New Testament, which were written six or seven hundred years later. Once again, my faith is confirmed and strengthened when I realize the incredible, improbable truth of the Bible. How could writers so far separated by time and space be inspired to write the same things? I believe they had the same source of inspiration—the Holy Spirit of God. No other explanation makes sense to me. Dear reader, I hope that you are realizing the same truth. The Bible is the truth! Now let's look at what Ezekiel wrote:

> I will give you a new heart and put a new spirit within you …
> I will put My Spirit within you
> Ezekiel 36:26-27

Now to the question "transformed into what? Transformed into your original self that God intended when He created you. I guess I should say transformed *back* into yourself. That's not really so bad, is it? The "new" you is really going to be the original you—the you that was, before the world and life pounded you into something else. God is simply offering to bring you back to the wonderful, kind, loving, happy, peaceful child you were born to be. God wants you to be happy. He wants you to live a life of love, peace, joy, and fulfillment. In fact, it is the "perfect will of God" that you "be transformed" into one who is living a new and improved life. He just told you how to achieve it—by renewing your mind. How do you renew your mind? By studying God's word, and asking Him to reveal His truth to you. When you ask Him in faith, He will reveal His truth for your life. As I've been researching the Bible for this book, I've been amazed at how true it is that the answers to just about any issue in life can be found in the word of God.

Until you gain your new and improved mind with its new and improved understanding and perspectives, you will continue in all the old habits and patterns that have characterized your life up until now. If your thought patterns don't change, it is not reasonable to expect that your life will change. Fill your mind with the truth of God—that is, godly, loving thoughts—and you will live a godly, loving life. Fill your mind with anything else, and well, you will get what you get.

Obviously, you cannot change your gender, race, birthplace, birth date, or your blood relatives (parents, siblings, etc.). However, what you *can* change is what you are going to make of your life from this moment on. You can choose to live a life of happiness, fulfillment, peace, and love, or you can choose to live a life of unhappiness, worry, stress, and fear—the choice is up to you.

First of all, you've been given the extraordinary gift of being born as a human being. You may not have ever thought about this, but as humans, we are the only one of the thousands of species of life forms on this planet that has the intellect and free will to determine our own personal destiny by the choices we make. We are not limited to living only by instinctual reaction to our environment.

Further, you have been blessed just to be able to read this. We all tend to take so many of our blessings for granted, as though they are our right to possess in the first place. No, they are not our right, they are privileges and gifts. It is by the grace of God that we were born into situations and circumstances in which we can enjoy these blessings, even the simple blessing of literacy. So many people in this world will never know the great joy of reading. I'm saying all this just to remind you, and myself for that matter, that even when things seem to be pretty gloomy, we still are incredibly blessed in so many wonderful ways. Rather than complaining, we should be giving thanks every day for our lives. Thank you, Lord!

We are the masters of our own destinies. But tragically, many people live as though they are the victims of their own lives. They don't realize that God has blessed them with the ability to choose whatever they want to become, to be as happy as they've always wanted to be, and to experience deep fulfillment in their lives. The only thing that's stopping them is themselves. The problem is they've been living under the influence of a lack of understanding of the truth. They've been deceived by lies that have robbed them of the realization of their birthright as blessed children of God. God has given all of us the right to choose to live our lives in a state of happiness, love, and abundance. Jesus said:

> "I have come that they might have life,
> and that they might have it more abundantly".
> John 10:10

This brings up an important point. When God is talking about abundance, He is not talking about what people usually think about when they think of abundance—a lot of money and material possessions. When God speaks of abundance, He is talking about an abundance of faith, hope, and love in our lives. God places His value on things of the heart and of the spirit. He knows that those are the things that bring true happiness, peace, and fulfillment to our lives.

I learned an important lesson about happiness and abundance when I was in high school and I was working as a lifeguard during the summers before and after my senior year. It made a very big impression on me. During my first summer as a lifeguard, I worked at a community pool in a blue collar neighborhood. Those people didn't have a lot of money, but I noticed that on the whole, they were kind, compassionate, friendly people who really cared about each other and who seemed to genuinely enjoy life. There were many neighborhood picnics and gatherings all summer long. In stark contrast, during my second summer as a lifeguard, I worked at a community pool in a very wealthy neighborhood. Those people seemed to be unhappy and for the most part, they were not enjoyable to be around. They appeared arrogant and self-absorbed. Their earthly abundance—money, big homes, and expensive cars—certainly did not bring them happiness. Even then, as a very young man, I was acutely aware of the difference in the two groups of people. God was teaching me what truly matters in life – what brings happiness and what doesn't. He was letting me witness firsthand that happiness comes from inside us, not from what we can accumulate outside of us.

While I'm thinking about it, I want to throw in a quick aside. One of the most incorrectly spoken clichés is the one about money. Most people say, "Money is the root of all evil" The correct statement is this: "The *love* of money is the root of all evil." That is a very critical distinction to realize. Money is an inert, impersonal tool. It is neither good nor evil. It simply is. Man's thoughts and emotions as related to money are what determine if money is used for good or evil. I'm not sure why, but I felt the need to clear up that issue. Perhaps someone will read that and receive a message.

God has given you the wonderful gift of personal choice in your life. Of course, if you're like most of us, some of your choices may not have turned out so well. However, it is because God does love us that He gave us that right to choose. If He controlled every step we make, then He wouldn't be loving at all. He'd be a dictator, and we'd be human robots. God knows that as we make our choices, we are going to make mistakes. That is how we learn. The operative word here is *learn*. Hopefully, through our experiences, we learn what works for us, what doesn't, what is important, and what isn't.

When you entered this world, your mind was a blank slate. Over the course of your life, you have accumulated many ideas, thoughts, and beliefs. Some of them are positive and encouraging; others are negative and discouraging, even destructive. But here is an important point to realize. If you can add thoughts to your mind, then of course, you can also delete them, and replace them. In fact, when you discard thoughts, you must replace them with something. Nature abhors a vacuum. When you get rid of undesirable, negative thoughts, something will come into your mind to fill the void. You must make the choice as to what those new thoughts will be. This is your chance to choose to fill your mind with positive, confident, loving thoughts—thoughts born of God's truth and His will for your life. That is why it is so absolutely critical that you turn to the word of God to be sure that you are learning the truth, the *real* truth. What kinds of things should you be thinking about to have a right mind? Paul, in his letter to the Philippians, told us precisely what we should think about.

> Finally, brethren, whatever things are true,
> whatever things are noble,
> whatever things are just, whatever things are pure,
> whatever things are lovely, whatever things are of good report,
> if there is any virtue and if there is anything praiseworthy—
> meditate on these things
> Philippians 4:8

There are many philosophies out there that are vying for your attention. Some of them appear quite appealing. However, if they are not consistent with God's word and His truth, they will eventually mislead you into dark and dangerous places. Cults are full of people who went searching for the "truth" and were deceived by false teachers and false doctrines. When in doubt, compare any philosophy, religion, or doctrine with the word of God. If whatever you are looking into is inconsistent with or conflicts with the word of God, reject it; you could be headed for trouble. Jesus warned us about false and deceiving teachers and doctrines.

> Beware of false prophets, who come to you in sheep's clothing,
> but inwardly they are ravenous wolves. You
> will know them by their fruits.
> Matthew 7:15

> "Then if anyone says to you, 'Look, here is the Christ!'
> or 'There!' do not believe it.
> For false christs and false prophets will rise
> and show great signs and wonders
> to deceive, if possible, even the elect.
> See, I have told you beforehand."
> Matthew 24:23-25

Dear reader, please take Jesus' words seriously. He warned us because He knows how easy it is for us to be deceived and He also knows the eternal consequences if we follow false teachers and their teachings.

God, through the apostle Paul, talked about the renewing of the mind as the way to transform yourself, because it is in the mind that thoughts are formed, and thoughts are what create our lives. When we make the effort to fill our minds with God's word and His truth, we change our lives back to God's original plan and we set ourselves on the straight and narrow path to salvation and eternity in Heaven with our glorious, loving God and Creator—our heavenly Father. One day, I look forward to seeing you there!

†

CLOSING THOUGHTS

A Fond Farewell

W ell, dear reader, I believe I've come to the end of what I wanted to discuss with you. It's kind of a strange feeling to come to the end. Do you recall what it was like when you came to the end of a trip with a group from school, or some other organization? You shared special moments, created memories, and formed some bonds. You became connected with those persons in a unique way through the experience of the journey. That's how I feel right now. For a brief period, we've been connected by these truths. I've enjoyed writing about them, and I sincerely hope that you've enjoyed reading about them. I pray that you've gained some insights into the truth of God, and that you will be blessed by God as you grow in His grace.

As you continue on your journey of discovering the truth, you will learn many things, and you will accumulate a lot of knowledge. My sincere hope and prayer for you is that with your knowledge, you will acquire wisdom.

For wisdom is better than rubies,
And all the things one may desire cannot be compared with her.
Proverbs 8:11

When you live in the wisdom of God's truth, you will find your purpose, your reason for being. Only then can you truly live out your part in God's great plan. And as you acquire God's wisdom, you will be able to pass it on to others, thereby helping them to find their truth and their destiny. I believe that is our ultimate duty—to serve and help others. We are all linked in this life. You've heard the phrase, "No man is an island." It is such a simple but profound truth. We were created to live and work and love together. Alone, we are for the most part out of sync with the rhythm of life. However, together, we can draw on the strengths and talents and abilities of each other for the betterment of all of us. As we give of ourselves to others, we usually find that somehow, we've grown and gained in ways we never expected. If we act only in our own best interests, we isolate ourselves and miss our purpose, and then the whole of mankind is weakened. We need each other for support and encouragement so we can interact synergistically to complete the design of God's creation.

I would very much like to receive your feedback on this book, and any other thoughts that you'd like to share. My email address is:

geoffguy13@gmail.com

I hope you will write and share some of your story with me. I plan on writing another book in which I want to share people's stories about how they came to accept Jesus as their Savior and how He has worked in their lives. We can all grow in our faith as we hear of the things that God has done for others. Many people have been blessed by God in many wonderful ways, some quite miraculous. I'd like to share some of those stories. I believe they would offer hope to others who may be struggling and need some reassurance that God is still out there and in the business of helping people.

Thank you for reading my book. I look forward to hearing your story. May God bless you and keep you in health and happiness.

Geoff